PRAISE FOR

Free Yourself to Love

"When I think of what I have learned from the message of biblical forgiveness I heard from Jackie Kendall, I think of going from being a prisoner in the jail of bitterness to being a free citizen in the country of grace. Jackie's message has been instrumental in my life many times. Forgiveness is not a suggestion, it is a command, and I know personally why God desires for us to forgive, forgive, forgive."

—*Jon Kitna, NFL quarterback*

"I am so thankful that Jackie Kendall chose to answer God's call and bare her life's struggles for the benefit of others. Because of her willingness to forgive, and her greater willingness to train others that forgiveness is a vital ingredient for spiritual growth, people like me can experience peace and harmony at home. My husband is no longer bound by the bitterness and hatred that he once carried."

—*Kim Singletary, wife of NFL Hall of Famer Mike Singletary*

"My heart has been challenged and changed by Jackie's powerful, unrelenting, persuasive message of forgiveness—no matter what, no matter who, no matter where! If you dare to pick up the gauntlet she has thrown down, you will be changed, too. Do it! You will never be sorry."

—*Jan Silvious, conference speaker and author of*
Big Girls Don't Whine *and* Smart Girls Think Twice

"FREE YOURSELF TO LOVE unlocks the mystery of true forgiveness. Jackie Kendall masterfully explains that forgiveness is not an automatic 'knee-jerk' response we need to offer as Christians but a process that involves acknowledgment of the hurt inflicted by the offense and a purposeful choice to quit being a hostage to shame, to the memories of the past, and to the incubation of anger. The principles in this book will set you free! I highly recommend it!"

—*Carol Kent, speaker and author of*
When I Lay My Isaac Down *and* A New Kind of Normal

"Jackie has more wisdom for us on the subject of love. She thoughtfully takes the reader on a journey deep into the rich topic of forgiveness and its implications for the human heart. I recommend this book for anyone longing for release from resentment and desiring the freedom to love."

—*Kristin Armstrong, author of*
Happily Ever After *and* Work in Progress

"Get your highlighters out and get ready to dog-ear some pages, folks. Jackie's trademark style had me laughing, crying, and pumping my fist in the air over the countless captives who will, no doubt, be set free. Every home should have multiple copies of this book on hand in their first-aid kits as a much-needed salve for broken and bruised hearts. Thank you, Jackie Kendall, for allowing God to take the pain of your past and use it to help others for His good and glory."

—*Vicki Courtney, bestselling author of*
Your Girl *and* TeenVirtue

"This is Jackie's greatest work yet. You only get liberating truth like this from having lived it. Hers is a story of unspeakable offense and unfathomable forgiveness. This book is for everyone who has been held hostage by unforgiveness."

—*Lisa Ryan, author, speaker, and host,*
EveryDay with Marcus & Lisa, *FamilyNet*

"Over the twenty-plus years of our friendship and ministry together, I've watched Jackie Kendall live what she teaches. I've listened as she clearly unpacks the biblical mandate for forgiveness. I've experienced the impact she has had on the lives of pro athletes, businesspeople, spouses, and coaches as they follow her intentional example. Jackie has gone ahead of most of us and demonstrates the Father's pleasure and grace in a life of trust and obedience. Read this book, consider its truth, then step out!"

—*Bobbe Evans, executive director of*
Pro Athletes Outreach and Coaches Time Out

JACKIE KENDALL

Free
Yourself
to Love

The Liberating Power of Forgiveness

New York Boston Nashville

Unless otherwise noted, Scripture quotations are taken from the HOLY BIBLE:
NEW INTERNATIONAL VERSION®. Copyright © 1973, 1978, 1984 by
International Bible Society. Used by permission of Zondervan Publishing House.
All rights reserved.

Scriptures noted KJV are taken from the King James Version of the Bible.

Scriptures noted NASB are taken from the New American Standard Bible®,
Copyright © 1960, 1962, 1963, 1968, 1972, 1975, 1977, 1995 by
The Lockman Foundation. Used by permission.

Scriptures noted NKJV are taken from the NEW KING JAMES VERSION.
Copyright © 1979, 1980, 1982, Thomas Nelson, Inc., Publishers.

Scriptures noted NLT are taken from the *Holy Bible*, New Living Translation,
copyright © 1996, 2004. Used by permission of Tyndale House Publishers, Inc.,
Carol Stream, Illinois 60188. All rights reserved.

Scriptures noted THE MESSAGE are taken from The Message. Copyright © 1993, 1994,
1995, 1996, 2000, 2001, 2002. Used by permission of NavPress Publishing Group.

FaithWords
Hachette Book Group
237 Park Avenue
New York, NY 10017

Visit our Web site at www.faithwords.com.

Printed in the United States of America

First Edition: February 2009
10 9 8 7 6 5 4 3 2 1

FaithWords is a division of Hachette Book Group, Inc.
The FaithWords name and logo are trademarks of Hachette Book Group, Inc.

Library of Congress Cataloging-in-Publication Data

Kendall, Jackie, 1950–
    Free yourself to love : the liberating power of forgiveness / Jackie Kendall. — 1st ed.
        p. cm.
    ISBN: 978-0-446-58089-2
    1. Forgiveness—Religious aspects—Christianity.   I. Title.
    BV4647.F55K44 2009
    234'.5—dc22

                            2008017903

To
Liz Minnick, my kindred-spirit friend,
who lived passionately committed
to the Great Forgiver;

and to
Ruth Allderige Olsen, my invaluable life coach and writing
mentor!

Contents

Contents

Part III

Escape for Hostages Who Want to Be Free

Acknowledgments

First and foremost, I want to give all praise to my Lord and Savior, Jesus Christ, who freely forgave me and taught me principles of forgiveness that healed my deeply wounded heart. His extravagant grace has transformed me into a wounded healer.

My editor, Holly Halverson, called this book my "magnum opus." Something so critically expressed in print needed the best of editors, and I am so grateful for Holly.

Thanks also to:

Ruth A. Olsen, my invaluable writing mentor, who held up emotional pom-poms, cheering me on as I struggled and wept through this manuscript. She was like a wise midwife for the birthing of this "magnum opus."

My agent, Leslie Nunn Reed, whose consistent flow of wisdom and kindness helps keep me focused and intentional about writing as an incomparable ministry.

So many people who courageously shared their struggles with forgiveness: Sophia, A.W., Alicia, Nancy, Leslie, Tim, Barb,

Diane, Christina, Courtney, Ruth, Linda, Mary Lou, Katrina, Chris, Andrew, Jon Kitna, and Mike Singletary.

Dear friends who have prayed for this message to finally be in print—especially DeDe, Vicki, Bettye, Ruth, LeeAnn, Sandy, Linda, and our dear Liz, who is now with the Great Forgiver, Jesus.

My two children, whom God has used for almost three decades to remind me of my need to let Jesus heal me so they don't have to carry my pain. They are daily mirrors reminding me to let God heal the past so that they and others don't have to keep paying in the present for my past heart wounds.

Last but not least, my husband of thirty-five years, who has forgiven me freely as I have been working out my "madness" in our marriage. He tells people constantly that we are married and still loving it because we are both good forgivers.

Introduction

I was reading through the workshop notes of a presentation on forgiveness given on September 7, 2006, to the United Nations and began to ponder the privilege of giving such a presentation. Suddenly, I realized that this book is my presentation to an entity even bigger and more influential than the UN: the huge family of God throughout the world. This book is my UN, my Ultimate Necessity presentation, written with the sole agenda of encouraging my brothers and sisters to walk in a daily lifestyle of forgiveness. Forgiveness is the call to love, and one can't love without the developed skill of forgiving freely.

I have read so many inspiring stories of forgiveness by people like Elie Wiesel, Corrie ten Boom, Doris Van Stone, Immaculée Ilibagiza, and many more. Whether a person survived a concentration camp, childhood abuse, or even what seems like a marginal offense (a rude remark, a harsh criticism, unfair comparisons), there are common principles these individuals applied to walk in such liberating freedom. I have been teaching these principles for two decades, and when exposed to them, people in every audience have said, "I didn't even realize that unforgiveness was free-floating in my soul." These principles come from the handbook given to us by the One who made forgiveness a possibility. Based on the greatest book of forgiveness, God's Word, I am sharing the practical nuts and bolts of forgiving as a way of life.

I also want to explain how I came to understand and practice this forgiving way of life. Everyone every day faces circumstances and offenses that require forgiveness. Some of our circumstances are more intensive or ongoing than others; in my life, the most acute offense God has taught me to forgive has been the repeated emotional and sexual abuse perpetrated upon me as a child by my father. I have had to face not only my own abuse, but also that of some of my siblings, two of whom took their own lives because of the agonizing pain they could not escape. What the Lord has taught me about the need for and the process of forgiving the most seemingly unforgivable offense is what I bring to you in this writing. Because my background of abuse has been my PhD-level of study in this arena, I will refer to it throughout this book.

Forgiving others reflects our understanding that we forgive because Jesus has forgiven us. Brennan Manning gives a poignant picture of Christ's forgiveness in action:

> Think again of forgiveness. In our hearts none of us have completely forgiven our enemies the way we should. In Jesus' post-Resurrection encounter with the apostles on the beach...when one might have expected, as Raymond Brown says, "the impact of unbearable glory," Jesus serves fish and chips. There is no mention, apparently

even no memory, of their betrayal. Never a reproach or even an indirect reference to their cowardice in the time of testing. No sarcastic greeting like, "Well, my fair-weather friends...." No vindictiveness, spite or humiliating reproach. Only words of warmth and tenderness.[1]

We must consider the depth of God's mercy and forgiveness to measure our own response in being good forgivers. A Christian who is not a good forgiver is an oxymoron. Love is one of the key characteristics a follower of Jesus should display, and forgiveness is a synonym for love. Whether you read the Old Testament or the New Testament, to be a great lover is to be a great forgiver: "The Lord our God is merciful and forgiving, even though we have rebelled against him" (Dan. 9:9).

We are called to forgive as our Father forgives: like Father, like son, like daughter. Our unwillingness to forgive is grievous to our Father, who paid such a high price to forgive us. When looking at God's mercy, we must always conclude that God is "gi-normous" in mercy: "Thou, Lord, art good, and ready to forgive" (Ps. 86:5 KJV).

In the Garden of Gethsemane, Jesus prayed that we would be *one* (see John 17:21). Then Jesus died a heinous death so that His blood would cleanse anything that challenged our oneness. This book is my contribution to encouraging the oneness among God's children Jesus prayed for in the garden. Oneness is possible when we have learned how to forgive one another for doing what we do best—being human.

In contrast, however, living in a state of unforgiveness toward one another is like the amputation of a part of our souls—as individuals and as a body. I fear that too often the church is more concerned about rules and ethics than this debilitating amputation. Yet it is critical to remember that we are most like Jesus not through our attempts to be perfect, but through our choices to forgive as we have been freely forgiven. I am a window display of the disposition of Jesus *when I am forgiving.*

The Bible tells us that as Christians we are new creations in Christ. Our identity is grounded in Him. If you are most like Jesus when you are forgiving, then a fundamental aspect of your identity is your ability and willingness to forgive. Think about that now: you may identify yourself as a mother, as a Southerner, as a football fan, or as a night owl. But if you identify yourself as a Christian, then who you are, who you strive to be, is one who forgives. Have you ever considered that your spiritual condition is reflected in this identity as one who forgives or, by contrast, one who chooses not to forgive?

Forgiveness is a complex topic, and to become identified as one who forgives is not a simple accomplishment. This book will examine in detail the excuses that run through our souls when we refuse to make the faith-filled choice of forgiving. I will also expose the dangerous condition that develops when one chooses to live in unforgiveness. This book contains practical instruction for developing skilled responses to the skilled inventions of the enemy of our souls, instruction intended not for the fainthearted but for those who are tired of being outwitted by the scheme of unforgiveness.

My desire for this book is that the comfort and compassion of Father God will flow into your heart, and you will no longer avoid dealing with the unforgiveness stashed away there! Let's be honest: we all offend in many ways, and we all need to be forgiven. Forgiving is like bringing in a cleanup crew for the damaged landscape in our souls after a relational storm.

I am not offering a superficial treatment for mortal heart wounds (see Jer. 6:14). But for those who have the courage to seek a deep healing for wounds, whether recent or ancient, I offer all that God has shown me.

Part I

The Lies That Bind
the Hostage

Chapter 1

Counterfeit Forgiveness

As I have stood at podiums and on stages throughout the past seventeen years teaching on unforgiveness, I have observed a very interesting phenomenon. Whether I am teaching professional athletes, a roomful of lawyers, or an audience packed with teenagers, I see many people leaning back in their chairs with their arms crossed. Their very body language says, "I do not have any unforgiveness in my heart." But then, as I begin to describe heart wounds, the characteristics of denial and excuses, and the principles of the freedom gained in forgiving, I see arms move from chests to laps. Next, people begin to lean forward in their chairs, their eyes widening in attentiveness.

What is happening? I believe what takes place is the resurrection of suppressed hurt and unforgiveness. Then the audience learns how to meet that pain as I tell them of the comfort I received through learning how to forgive my offender. This comfort overflows into the hearts of the listeners.

To forgive or not to forgive: that is the question. For the

follower of Jesus, the answer is always the same—to forgive is the only choice. When a person hesitates to forgive another, it is not just a personal soul-care issue, or an issue of personality, culture, ethnicity, education, or social status. This reticence flows from reasoning influenced by a skillfully devised scheme. Who is behind this skillfully devised scheme? None other than the devil himself, the very enemy of our souls.

Let's look more closely at this formidable scheme in our Christian walk.

The Schemer

Paul wrote,

> If you forgive anyone, I also forgive him. And what I have forgiven—if there was anything to forgive—I have forgiven in the sight of Christ for your sake, *in order that Satan might not outwit us. For we are not unaware of his schemes.* (2 Cor. 2:10–11, emphasis added)

Paul, the greatest apostle, wrote that Satan schemes to outwit God's children through the relational crime of unforgiveness. When I hesitate to forgive, not only am I struggling emotionally, but I have stepped onto the "outwitting" battlefield of the adversary. Paul mentions in this passage that "we are not unaware of his schemes." I believe that many of God's children are, in fact, outwitted daily because of their ignorance of Satan's grand scheme to keep us from forgiving.

Consider this reality: *the blood of Jesus purchased for us the unspeakable privilege of forgiveness as well as the miraculous gift of being identified as people not only forgiven but also people who forgive.*

Satan is a mastermind. A word-for-word translation of

2 Corinthians 2:11 powerfully expresses this fact: "So that we not be over-reached by Satan, because we are absolutely not ignorant of the way he exercises his mind."[1] The Hebrew word for "exercises" refers to the exercise of the mind in order to plan something.[2] Believers who are ignorant of these active plans are easily outwitted by the adversary of our souls.

It doesn't stop there. When Satan outwits us, he has demonstrated two of his most familiar exploitations. First, he tempts us to be unforgiving. Then, when we become cemented in our refusal to forgive, this adversary moves from tempter to accuser. Consider this: if you have hesitated to forgive someone in your life and that hesitation then becomes permanent, not only have you been tempted and outwitted, you have actually given the accuser his ammunition (see Rev. 12:10)!

Reasons We Don't Forgive

We can be tragically ignorant about this skillful invention of the enemy, these excuses to not forgive. We forget that the native tongue of the devil is lies (see John 8:44). Too often we think our hesitation to forgive is emotionally based. Rarely do we pause and consider that the original liar is coaching us with these excuses.

I was on the phone one day talking with a precious Christian friend. She mentioned meeting a dear friend in secret. Why the secrecy? Do they live in a city where their religious freedom is threatened? No. They were meeting in secret because of the estrangement between their godly husbands. What caused this serious breach in the friendship? Was it heresy? Was it an immoral offense? No. The conflict was over the use of a particular translation of the Bible and cruel, judgmental remarks.

This situation is not exceptional, but it is so sad when placed in the context of Jesus' prayer for His future children. Jesus purchased a capacity for forgiveness for each of His children. When Christians disagree and become estranged, it is not just an issue of clashing perspectives—it is an issue of pride-resistant unforgiveness. The unspeakable privilege of having a personal relationship with Jesus is casually minimized when any of God's kids are outwitted by the enemy of their souls through the all-too-familiar behavior of unforgiveness.

> If anyone claims, "I am living in the light," but hates a Christian brother or sister, that person is still living in darkness. Anyone who loves another brother or sister is living in the light and does not cause others to stumble. (1 John 2:9–10 NLT)

The more I thought about the offense and the breakup of this godly friendship, the more I grieved the callousness that allows so many Christians to live day in and day out with unforgiving hearts toward other Christian brothers and sisters. Even among God's most mature children, one can witness the drama of unforgiveness—unloving behavior toward a spiritual sibling. What about the simple remark Jesus made at the Last Supper: "*All men* will know that you are my disciples, if you love one another" (John 13:35, emphasis added)?

We deny having unforgiving hearts and defy promptings to address the offenses. But we don't recognize that the very thing we engage in as self-protection is the mind-set that actually keeps us in bondage. We are held hostage by the "lies that bind." What I see transpiring from the podium when I speak on forgiveness is the loosening of these bonds.

Jesus said that offense would come. You have been offended.

Offend means "to create anger, resentment, annoyance, hurt the feelings of someone."[3] The last time you were offended, how did you respond emotionally? Consider the effective out-witting that persists—constantly—in our minds and hearts in the area of forgiveness.

In this chapter, I want to reveal a very common yet emotionally unhealthy manner in which people respond to being offended or hurt. Rather than moving toward the healing act of forgiveness, we have a strong tendency to engage in *counterfeit forgiveness*. This form of emotional denial does not heal the offense; it actually intensifies the impact of the harm done by the offender.

The Forms of Counterfeit Forgiveness

What are these lies that bind, the lies of counterfeit forgiveness? In general, they are denied or repressed feelings. Such denial manifests in these forms: stoic numbness, minimizing the wrong, psychoanalyzing the offender, emotionally holding your breath, and avoiding by being an overachiever. These kinds of counterfeit forgiveness fool us into thinking that we have dealt with our hurt or anger, but really, we have just masked the pain.

Just as the memory of Christ's death for our sins must be proclaimed, so also the memory of human suffering must be made public. Rosa Luxembourg, a Polish reformer, said, "The most revolutionary deed is and always will remain to *say out loud what is the case.*"[4] I am speaking out against the tyranny of keeping one's hurts and pains hidden underground and burying the best part of oneself! Secrecy is the power that keeps so many captive. Learning to forgive is the means of being set free.

Counterfeit #1: Stoic Numbness

Let's begin with the condition of stoic numbness. Some consider it a strength to deal stoically with loss, trauma, hurt, disappointment, or shattered dreams. Too many Christians have the misconception that great faith means an almost wooden response to suffering. Nothing could be farther from the truth.

Stoic numbness is actually unhealthy. When one person has been offended by another and he responds by sucking it up and becoming numb, such controlled emotions deny the impact of the offense. I heard a pastor say years ago that the source of most emotional and spiritual ills is an *inappropriate effort to avoid pain*. Stoic numbness is one of the methods we use to avoid pain. Forgiveness, on the other hand, requires processing raw experience. This book will help you move from detached, numb stoicism into the healing freedom of biblical forgiveness.

One typical characteristic of stoicism is a *rush to forgive* without taking time to feel the trauma and pain. In an "emotional coma," one avoids doing the hard work of processing the different stages that follow trauma. We've all heard about the stages of grief: shock (the "emotional coma"), denial, anger (rage), bargaining, and then finally acceptance and forgiveness. The following e-mail is an example of a precious young girl who rushed to forgive a man who drugged and raped her during her first semester at college.

> *Hey, Jackie,*
> *My mom told me that you had heard about what had happened this past weekend. I just wanted to let you hear from me that I'm doing okay. God Is Good!! Things could have been so much worse than what they are. I don't remember anything*

that happened to me, therefore the emotional pain is not as great as it could be, and I am not physically hurt whatsoever. I have done nothing but praise God since this happened. I know how great He is and I know that what happened, happened for a reason. I'm not saying that the devil didn't have anything to do with this, but we WILL come out on top of this and justice will be served. I hear that a lot of people are extremely angry about what happened. I wish I could show them that anger doesn't solve anything. Although I do want justice to be served and I want whoever would do such an evil thing to me to be caught, I hold no anger.

This dear young woman rushed to forgive as her upbringing and training encouraged her to do. Emotional numbness is evident, though, in her remarks about not being angry and that anger serves no purpose. She was not feeling anger because she was in the first stage of a trauma—an emotional coma! Just around the corner from that coma was anger, and it became apparent in many painful choices that the traumatized victim began to make. Yes, the reality that a victim can't rush forgiveness was displayed months later when she started to make painful choices that revealed a repressed heart wound.

Sometimes stoicism takes the form of putting on a face for the sake of others. After Martin Luther King Jr. was killed, no one in his immediate family—neither Coretta Scott King nor her four little children—was seen crying in public. Not only did Mrs. King mask her grief when she was in the public eye, she dove right back into work, leading a march in Memphis quite soon after her husband's funeral. She would go on to regret her stoicism, citing its great cost, and told *People* magazine: "I don't think in the end it's a good idea, because eventually the grief has to come out."[5]

"The grief has to come out." We put on our masks and try to protect ourselves and others, but often the Lord has another plan. We have all heard the expression "You are only as sick as your secrets." I believe the Lord wants His children to not waste so much energy and emotion trying to disguise the heart wounds they carry.

A perfect picture of this was shown me in the Scriptures:

> The king of Israel said to Jehoshaphat, "I will enter the battle in disguise, but you wear your royal robes."...When the chariot commanders saw Jehoshaphat, they thought, "Surely this is the king of Israel." So they turned to attack him, but when Jehoshaphat cried out, the chariot commanders saw that he was not the king of Israel and stopped pursuing him. But someone drew his bow at random and hit the king of Israel between the sections of his armor. (1 Kings 22:30, 32–34)

The king of Israel went into battle disguised so he would be sure to dodge the attack of the enemy, but a random soldier with a random arrow pierced through the disguise of the king. The lesson? God, in His sovereignty, pierces our disguises.

Our disguises and the secrets we attempt to hide are as varied as we are. My mother was molested as a child, and her survival technique consisted of humor and good works. Humor and good works enabled her to supply constant entertainment and stay in perpetual motion, so that her children could not sustain her attention long enough for her to grasp the gravity of what a predator we had as a father. Scripture says of such people, "They are absorbed in their own pain and grief" (Job 14:22 NLT).

When someone's disguise is the kind of stoicism that represses and denies a painful past, that pain may not reliably remain underground. Often, it will resurrect at the most inopportune times—and in ways that can utterly confuse other people! For example, a misunderstanding between two people may not necessarily flow from an offending incident but from repressed hurt and offenses. Dr. Aloys von Orelli, a psychotherapist, said, "We are irritated by that in others which we have repressed in ourselves."[6]

For years there was terrible tension between my mother-in-law, Esther, and me. (Okay, I know, that might not shock some people!) This tension was not typical. It was as if she were at war with the *good* in my life. As I was growing and courageously facing my heart wounds, whenever I would share something new I was learning, the tension just seemed to increase. Years later, I learned about the terrible childhood Esther had. That childhood pain was deeply repressed, and I was irritating the reality of the deeply hidden pain.

A friend wrote to me about the reasons she finds it hard to forgive:

> *I don't forgive because . . .*
> *It is easier to blame—it's a quick fix that gives me the feeling I am in control, especially if they don't apologize or realize they have hurt me. Blaming rather than forgiving gives me a false sense of security, confidence, and closure on the issue. But then I am allowing my feelings of bitterness, resentment, anger, etc., to control me.*

I feel too vulnerable when dealing with the issue.
I think I deserve better treatment from others.
I easily forget how much God has forgiven me.
I easily forget that God can heal hurts and do the impossible.

—*Alicia Murphy, Belfast*

Counterfeit #2: Minimization

A popular counterfeit of forgiveness is overlooking the wrong. This is where you minimize the offense. For example, when you hear a battered woman say, "He really didn't mean to push me through that door," or a mother say to her toddler, "Daddy didn't mean to yell at you," you are hearing classic minimizing. If he didn't mean it, then why did he do and say those things? Sometimes we think we're being forgiving when we look the other way. We think that's healthy, but it's not.

During an intense counseling session, I realized how much I had minimized what my father did to me as a teen. Minimizing is like putting a Band-Aid on cancer. Forgiving an incident without dealing with the root issue is like trying to paint over a rusty door. One must first sand the door, removing the rust, then paint the door. Here's a biblical example: When Joseph's brothers were finally reunited with him after they had sold him into slavery, he didn't minimize what they had done to him. He didn't say, "It's okay, guys! Look at the good that came out of it. God worked all things together for good!" No. While that was true, he actually said, "You *intended* to harm me, but God intended it for good" (Gen. 50:20, emphasis added)! Everybody always talks about how God worked out Joseph's victimization, but let's talk about what really happened to him as well. It was evil.

As Jacob was dying, his sons gathered around him to receive his final blessing. During the blessings, Jacob spoke of a crime committed by the brothers against the favored Joseph. Did Jacob keep everything light and lovely during his last moments with his sons? *No.* He exposed the crime, saying of Joseph: "With bitterness archers attacked him; they shot at him with hostility" (Gen. 49:23).

Jealousy in Joseph's brothers led to bitterness, and this bitterness resulted in their selling their younger brother into captivity. Jacob did not minimize what his sons did to their younger brother—even though God had worked things out for good. Jacob still addressed the relational crime committed.

True forgiveness is seeing something for what it really is; that's when you effectively forgive. When someone makes a rude remark and hurts your feelings, don't just say, "Never mind," when they ask you what is wrong. We think we're forgiving if we say, "Oh no, it's nothing." That in itself is wrong. Do not minimize the offense by overlooking it in an effort to appear merciful and patient. In fact, we need to pay greater attention to what motivates us to overlook an offense. Sometimes fear motivates us not to say how we are actually hurt. It is even possible that we want to *seem* forgiving to another, because, after all, we are *Christians*, but really that is our pride at work.

Minimization also allows for what Dr. Aaron Lazare has titled *trash apologies*. Trash apologies contain phrases like these:

- Mistakes were made. (Rather than "I made a mistake.")
- To the degree you were offended...(Rather than "To the degree I offended you.")

- If I did anything wrong...("If" as opposed to "I did something wrong.")
- You can't expect me to be perfect.
- If I've hurt anybody, I'm sorry. (Again, "If" as opposed to "I've hurt you, and I'm sorry.")
- I'm sorry you are mad. (But I am not responsible for your being mad.)[7]

Counterfeit #3: Psychoanalyzing the Offender

Another method people use to minimize an offense is to psychoanalyze the people who offend them. I also call this *pity-based analysis*, and it's just another form of denial. We are too quick to explain away foul behavior with excuses—people had a bad day, they were stressed by having in-laws in town for a week, or they overreacted because of the wounds of their childhoods. My mother used to defend my father's nocturnal visits to my bedroom as his way of wanting to feel "close" to me. Talk about psychoanalyzing!

The problem, once again, is that instead of achieving forgiveness, the issue just gets buried until finally you blow up like a volcano! Then people wonder what's wrong with you because they've never heard one thing about the buried offenses that have been building up.

Remember Jacob's deathbed scene? Jacob verbally acknowledged in front of those listening what the brothers actually did to Joseph. Many times in a family conflict you want to bring up what's really going on. But before you can get to what's happened, the other starts defending himself, or your parents say, "Come on now, we don't want an argument." Nothing ever gets resolved. You are never allowing anything to address the breach in these important relationships. Moreover, people hesitate to say anything against their parents, because the Bible tells us to "honor" them (Exod. 20:12 KJV). The word *honor* in Hebrew actually means "to recognize the weight of" or "weighty."[8] I eventually had to recognize the weight of the influence of my dysfunctional home and parents.

Too many times to number, I have listened to people minimize the abandonment they suffered through divorce. Divorce is epidemic, and the denial about the heart wound of abandonment is stunning. Whenever I hear a person say that he or she had an "amicable divorce," I'm shocked; believe me, the *children* of the divorce never felt it was amicable. We are too casual about the incredible pain that comes when spouses/parents separate. It is a terrible wound to be abandoned by someone who should have protected, led, and loved you. To minimize that wound usually leads to the offended spouse's or child's burying the hurt.

If you bury the hurt, you'll bury the hate, because believe it or not, where hurt comes, inevitably hate and anger come also. We don't want to admit these feelings, because we want to consider ourselves very loving, gentle, adaptable, kind, and wonderful. You know that when someone hurts you, the feeling afterward is not love. If you bury the hurt, you bury the hate, and then you bury the possibility of being healed. Healing comes only when we dig it out and let the Holy Spirit show us how to handle the offense.

Let's stop pushing these feelings down! The Father wants to take us by the hand and say, "Don't panic! I've got the best tools, and I can work that thing right out." For God, it is not a

---

problem; the problem is when we're covering it over and walking around like unapproachable ice-people, afraid someone might find out we're in pain.

Yet as Christians, we, if anybody, should be telling the truth. Jesus said in John 8:31–32, "If you continue in My word, then you are truly disciples of Mine; and you will know the truth, and the truth will make you free" (NASB). Let's not kid ourselves or one another. When someone asks, "How are you?" don't simply respond, "Fine." Be honest with yourself and others. Honesty brings hope for forgiveness.

When we minimize an offense, we inadvertently minimize the need to forgive and the price that Jesus paid for forgiveness. Do not minimize the Cross and what Jesus did for us. Let's put a stop to minimizing and psychoanalyzing. People offend because they're sinners and need help and accountability.

Counterfeit #4: Holding One's Breath Emotionally

As we have looked at a few kinds of counterfeit forgiveness—stoic numbness, minimizing wrongs done to you, and analyzing the offender—do you recognize any of these behaviors? I imagine you do! And I imagine you'll recognize this next one, too—how people sometimes "suck it up" emotionally. There are ways in which this is similar to stoicism, but the difference is that the stoic person might tend to put on a face for others to *cover up hurt feelings*, whereas holding your breath emotionally *doesn't even acknowledge the emotions* or make allowance for them. They are frozen, locked up in the deep freeze!

I went to dinner with a widow and she shared her story. When her husband realized he was dying, he wrote love letters that were to be delivered to her every Valentine's Day along with Godiva chocolates for not only his wife but each of his daughters. They had just passed their fifth Valentine's Day with a new letter and chocolates from her dead husband. I was so touched by this loving story...but then another tragic aspect was revealed: her mother had told this widow that she must not cry—and the widow had listened to her! I asked, "What do you do when you feel tears starting to erupt?" She shrugged her shoulders and quietly said, "I just hold my breath and they stop."

This poor woman was holding her breath, stopping normal emotions from flowing. And just as this mother gave her widowed daughter pathetic instruction, I have seen Christian leaders tell a person who has experienced deep offense to "just get over it." Being offended is like grief—both require a certain measure of emotion and time to process.

Too often when people hold their breath emotionally, they will use that other counterfeit, minimizing what has happened to them. Minimization allows the heart wound to take root and grow into something more deadly than the initial offense: bitterness. Minimization blocks your ability to see the offense as it really is and to forgive freely.

By admitting you've been hurt so deeply you hardly know how to communicate it, you free yourself from the bondage of that hurt. God designed women especially to be able to get in touch with the deepest part of their cores. Yet so many Christians desire to be "good," and in their minds that means never complaining or rocking the boat, while always smiling—"Praise the Lord anyway!"

Be specific. Everyone is always so afraid of being specific, yet the Cross was a very specific moment! Jesus drank a very specific cup in the garden when He cried and sweat blood over it. He drank every horrible thing that's ever touched your life. And the best part is that He wants to heal your wound so you can get over it and get on with life! But when we fail to admit our hurt, pain, and devastation in the name of faith, we are diminishing who Christ is and what He did for us.

Years ago I saw a movie called *The Prince of Tides*. The lead character was in a counseling session where he was describing the horrible night when he was a child and three escaped criminals broke into the family's home and raped all the children. When his mother came home and saw what was happening, she took a shotgun and gunned down the attackers. After killing those men, the mother cleaned up the blood and removed the criminals to be buried. The lead character in this movie, Tom, said, "Worse than the rape was the silence." None of the children were allowed to speak about the horror.

Holding one's breath emotionally only intensifies the pain. It takes so much courage to feel the pain and do the hard work of recovering from such deep offense.

As I have said before and will say again before this book is through, you begin to forgive when you state the specific wrong done to you. This isn't necessarily something that should be done publicly. Pick a small accountability group, a few close friends, or a trusted counselor to admit this to. I recognize there is a great fear of betrayal. I know this is hard, because Christians want to be real, open up, and tell where they're struggling—but many have had past experiences where they opened up to a godly person, maybe someone in leadership, and the person they trusted disclosed their private thoughts. Afterward, they shut down with a big lock on their inner feelings, never to be released again; the pain just rumbles all the time, like a granite-covered volcano. Before you can move on from the memory, your first step must be to acknowledge what's been done to you.

Silent minimization is a self-protective cover-up that has lethal ramifications. When I was in counseling in college, I learned that I handled my sexual abuse by minimizing it. I managed to successfully cover it up again until my sister Bobbie committed suicide in 1990—fifteen years later! Where did I hide my offense? I hid it under a pile of good works.

Counterfeit #5: Being an Overachiever

During my junior year, I volunteered to take a temperament analysis test. I couldn't wait to see my results. The administrators couldn't believe my results were accurate and even proposed I retake the test! I ranked incredibly high in the category of hostility. I cried when they told me, because I felt so much shame. But they said, "Jackie, you could not be this hostile unless you're hiding something." That's when a very wise woman asked, "Would you like to talk?" So I began to tell her about my dad.

As this kind lady listened to the heinous soul crime of sexual abuse I'd suffered, she just wept. Her tears caught me off guard—I had never wept for myself. Maybe her tears seem unprofessional to some, but to me, they were a demonstration of deep compassion. Through her tears she said something very important to me, based on 2 Corinthians 1:3–5. She assured me that the God of all comfort, if I would allow Him to comfort me in this horrible, damaged area of my life, would enable me to be a blessing to many people. I remember her saying,

"Jackie, there are so many people you're going to be able to encourage if you just let Jesus heal this hidden damage."

> All praise to God, the Father of our Lord Jesus Christ. God is our merciful Father and the source of all comfort. He comforts us in all our troubles so that we can comfort others. When they are troubled, we will be able to give them the same comfort God has given us. For the more we suffer for Christ, the more God will shower us with his comfort through Christ. (2 Cor. 1:3–5 NLT)

How destructive was this secret? It made me so hostile that on the temperament results graph, I was in the 99.9 percentile. Apparently I could have run that evaluation graph right off the paper! I came to understand that I hid my damage by becoming an overachiever—highly driven. I had to have straight As, had to do the best, had to be the best Christian, the best woman. I was trying to cover up all that damage through perfectionistic striving. In my mind, I was just driven to succeed, but what I didn't recognize was that I was driven to outrun the pain, hide it, and hide from it.

You may be reading this and thinking, *I was physically [or sexually] abused; I was neglected [or betrayed]. But I don't want to bring that stuff up again. I've dealt with it. I've moved on. It's not affecting my life.* What I want to ask you is, have you really dealt with your past? Have you processed past offenses with a godly counselor, and have you prayed through the hurt, whether shallow or deep? Because in fact, most people think they have dealt with such pain by just not thinking about it. You've decided that if you work harder and you run harder and you're more disciplined and more driven, you can drive it away. Or possibly you have learned to avoid the offense by lapsing into depression or addiction or a kind of numb passivity. Regardless of the method of avoidance, if you're attempting to bury the offense, it's likely you've buried it deep. And the deeper you bury it, the more acute and toxic the pain becomes.

Here is a critical thing to understand: a childhood offense may not resurrect in your latter teens or even your early twenties, but eventually it will arrive at your breakfast table. In adulthood, all the things that are hidden are finally revealed. At that point, the buried offense and your need to forgive will be revealed.

Offend Not Thyself Through the Denial of the Offense

In this chapter, I have illustrated some classic and tragic examples of the lies of counterfeit forgiveness. These are all ways we deny we were offended or minimize the depth of the pain from offense. Remember the definition of *offend*: to create anger, resentment, annoyance, hurt the feelings of someone. As Christians we can stop hiding the effects of our offenses and face them with courage, because we have the grace-given capacity to forgive. It's imperative to recall this as well: not only are we offended but we *all* offend—as long as there is breath in our bodies, we have this capacity. "In many things we offend all. If any man offend not in word, the same is a perfect man, and able also to bridle the whole body" (James 3:2 KJV).

Can you think of a time this week when someone offended you? Do the same people offend you on a regular basis? Are you easily offended? Do you offend others frequently? Being offended is not a rare experience but an inevitable reality since we live outside the Garden of Eden. Even Jesus spoke of such a reality: "It is impossible that no offenses should come, but woe to him through whom they do come!" (Luke 17:1 NKJV).

If we all offend and are offended regularly, it is critical we possess the tools to forgive. Consider the significance of Jesus' addressing this inevitability in the Lord's Prayer in Matthew 6: "Forgive us our debts, as we also have forgiven our debtors" (v. 12). If you say you have no one to forgive, you must live in an emotional vacuum or on a planet without contact with other humans!

Being Offended Is Inevitable; Staying Offended Is My Choice

Learning to become a good forgiver is the only road of release from the prison of offense. If one denies the offense, the imprisonment is lifelong. How many believers really grasp the agenda of the enemy of our soul that Jesus spoke about in John 10? How many of us consider that the battle inside we are committed to hiding is fueled by the cheering of the enemy? "The thief comes only to steal and kill and destroy; I have come that they may have life, and have it to the full" (John 10:10).

Life "to the full" includes release from the bondage of yesterday's offenses. God said of Jesus, "You will be a light to guide the nations. You will open the eyes of the blind. You will free the captives from prison, releasing those who sit in dark dungeons" (Isa. 42:6–7 NLT).

Jesus, the Light of the World, came not only to die for our sins but also to set us free from the dark dungeons of marinating offense. Unforgiveness is a cold, damp, dark dungeon from which all the trinkets and toys of the world will not be an effective distraction. Scripture says, "[God's] own people have been robbed and plundered, enslaved, imprisoned, and trapped" (Isa. 42:22 NLT). How often in just the past year have you been robbed of life to the full and trapped in a dark dungeon because of a marinating offense?

Forgiveness is the *processing* of a raw experience. For me, forgiveness has involved serious, faith-fueled "holy sweat." Not a day goes by without my needing to forgive — to overlook a grievance caused by an encounter with another human being. That is why Paul wrote, "Forgive whatever grievances [offenses] you may have against one another. Forgive as the Lord forgave you" (Col. 3:13).

We've seen that Jesus addressed forgiveness in the Lord's Prayer: "Forgive us our debts, as we forgive our debtors" (Matt. 6:12 KJV). The Greek word for "forgive" in this verse is *apheimi*, which means "send forth, forsake, lay aside, leave alone, omit, put away, remit, suffer, yield up."[9]

All the terms used to define forgiving are verbs — action words. Each of these refers to something that I am to *do* — to engage in actively — in response to being offended by someone else.

Throughout this book, you will learn many practical things to do in relation to being offended. The material in this book will help you maneuver through a loving response of forgiveness that will set you free: free to express unrealized amounts of mercy and love.

MAKE IT PERSONAL

Gather with some close friends and take this quiz. Afterward, discuss whether anyone was surprised by his or her results. If someone scores extremely high, talk about how that person has used counterfeit forgiveness, and how he or she can begin to process and forgive — and heal.

Rate Your Forgiveness

On a scale of 0–100, rate your forgiveness in the following situations:

25–50: It hurts to think about it, but you can disconnect fairly quickly.

51–75: The memory of the incident lingers most of the day.

76–90: You are enraged when you think of the event.

91–100: You hope the person burns in hell.

_____ Your parent said something to you that angers you each time you recall the incident.

_____ Someone you trusted owes you money.

_____ Someone you trusted took unfair advantage of you.

_____ Someone else got the raise or job you deserved.

_____ Someone told a lie about you.

_____ You can't forgive your spouse or significant other for...

_____ Your child or good friend totally disappointed you.

_____ You were treated badly in childhood.

_____ Someone you love cheated on you.

_____ You can't forgive yourself for...

_____ Total

Scoring:

Under 315 = Occasionally you may need to work on forgiveness.

315–450 = You have some significant forgiveness issues.

Anything over 450 is an indication of major unforgiveness.[10]

Chapter 2

Held Hostage by Shame

Forgiven,
Stamped by grace
Marked by love,
Love of God.
I've done the
Unspeakable,
Been shamed by
My human-ness
Yet I stand forgiven.
Take the freedom
That's handed to me.
How could I do any less
When He has Done
Mysteriously More.
                    —*Leslie Davies*[1]

I n chapter 1, we looked at counterfeit forgiveness and identified some examples of the habits that hold us hostage
to unforgiveness. I hope you recognized some of these
characteristics and that, like the men and women in the audiences I described, you are even beginning to notice a loosening
of some old bonds. There *is* freedom for the hostage! I have
witnessed it and experienced it.

Here is something else I have witnessed: when we begin this
process of being liberated from unforgiveness, a deeply buried pipeline fuels our inclination to deny our hurt feelings. I
spent years unaware of that fuel line. But when God brought in
the heavy machinery and we began to really rip into that deep
ground, do you know what I found? The fuel coursing through
that pipe was *shame*. And as long as that shame was operative,
as long as it was pumping through my soul, I fought all raw
emotion. Even worse than that, there was a vicious cycle going
on, because I came to learn that hiding and denying difficult
feelings actually fuels the shame.

Shame keeps us all entangled in the lies that bind and crip-
ples our capacity to walk in authentic forgiveness.

Adept at Hiding Emotions

People are adept at hiding their emotions, but as a consequence,
they are living with deep reserves of destructive shame. Shame
is the by-product of moving raw feelings underground. Rather
than bare our emotions to another encouraging believer, a professional counselor, or even to the Lord, we are shamed into
hiding our deep anguish. But hiding those emotions when you
have been offended actually doubles the consequences of the

offense! Not only do you have to experience the hurt of the offense, but you also have to embrace the dishonor of hiding what has happened. Shame assaults your esteem, so the offense has put a wedge not only between you and the offender but between you and your heart's true voice. Shame can even jam wedges between you and God. These wedges become bitter denial hidden under that "faith grin," that "game face."

Christians are called to bear one another's burdens. We are to encourage one another to face the shame of the past that robs us of the gifts of our present lives. How ironic it is that men or women who were sexually abused are full of shame—and yet they are the victims! They attempt to hide what happened as though hiding will help them recover. Wounds that are hidden only erode self-esteem through the screaming message of dishonoring shame. Spiritually a person needs the reminder that God is not in the business of shaming His kids. Only the enemy of our souls does this.

Jesus came to heal our heart wounds, yet shame keeps us prisoners of the original offense. In a sense, shame and unforgiveness team up to keep the offended one prisoner. Shame is a shadow over the unforgiving heart. It is the wound that keeps on wounding. Shame combined with unforgiveness allows what happened to me decades ago to intrude on the present and ruin my day. The only solution is to learn how to forgive past offenses so they can't constantly step with muddy footprints all over the present. The psalmist wrote, "Those who look to him for help will be radiant with joy; no shadow of shame will darken their faces" (Ps. 34:5 NLT).

The Role the Church Plays

The sad fact is that people's burying of hurt and feelings of shame is not necessarily accomplished in a vacuum. There is a systemic condition in the church—in human nature—in which we encourage one another in this destructive practice. In the book of Esther, one of the key characters, Mordecai, was in mourning. Because of this, he could not enter the palace:

> When Mordecai learned of all that had been done, he tore his clothes, put on sackcloth and ashes, and went out into the city, wailing loudly and bitterly. But he went only as far as the king's gate, because no one clothed in sackcloth was allowed to enter it. (Est. 4:1–2)

Those verses captured my attention as I thought about how uncomfortable people often are around someone who is grieving. Yet we as Christians are not to imitate the attitude of the heathen kings of old. Instead, we are to approach our heavenly King, to whom we can always come boldly, regardless of our condition—mourning or deliriously happy (see Heb. 4:15–16).

I have attended too many churches where the people were very uncomfortable with anything negative—like mourning and suffering. Therefore, these situations had to be handled quickly. People were not allowed to process grief at their own pace. They had to put on the happy face—what I call their "happy depression."

How thrilled I was, therefore, to witness a beautiful counterexample to that norm when my husband and I moved to a new church last year. The church had a special Sunday during the Christmas season to acknowledge all the people who had lost a loved one that year. It was called "Home for Christmas

Sunday." As the pastor began to explain to the newcomers the purpose of this special Sunday, Ken and I were touched beyond words expressible: "There are so many families in our church that have experienced the loss of a loved one this year. We know that Christmas will be particularly hard for each of you, and we want to pray with you and weep with you about this." The minister went on to say, "The church should be the one place that grief is safe to be expressed... again and again."

My husband and I wept as we saw hundreds go to the front of the church, where the pastor hugged each person and prayed with each family as the mourners were allowed to grieve openly. Every mourning family was given a special ornament to remind them throughout the holidays, whenever they were missing their loved ones, the loved ones were "home for Christmas."

Here is the opposite scenario. Years ago, in another church, a deacon was caught in a prostitution sting. He and his wife were brought in front of our congregation so he could acknowledge his adultery and she could admit her willingness to forgive him. I saw her a few days later and told her how sorry I was that she was pressured to forgive her husband in such a rush. I said, "You should have time to mourn the breaking of your marital covenant. You should wear black for as long as it takes!" But all she could do was to give me the "grin of faith" and walk away. This woman was not only rushed into forgiveness but was not allowed any time to process the grief of the betrayal and the public humiliation. The next time he was caught—they moved out of town.

It turned out that another man in our church was involved in the same prostitution sting. His wife was trying to follow the "rush to forgive" example of the deacon's wife. When she called to tell me, she said, "At first I was so mad that I threw all his clothes on the lawn and then I threw all his other stuff out! But then I decided I was going to forgive him and I went out and brought all his stuff back in."

I was glad she chose to forgive him, yet I was convinced that her rush to forgive involved skipping a step. To legitimately forgive, she needed to face her private thoughts and feelings, including the pain, anger, rage, and betrayal that came with finding out about her husband. Interestingly, she went on to share a revealing consequence of that rush to forgive: "Well, I was fine for a couple of days until I was doing laundry. I held up one of my little girl's dresses, and I thought, *I wonder what the prostitute looked like?* Then I burst into tears and was ready to throw his clothes right back out on the front lawn!"

Her denial of her deep hurt, the rush to forgive—covering deep hurt over with the "grin of faith"—ruptured later with a painful moment of tears in front of her girls. Quite frankly, to rush forgiveness is to trash forgiveness. To lightly dismiss any grievance that stirs us to deep anger is damaging. Offenses that are lightly brushed off as "no big deal" are rarely settled permanently. Certainly there are annoyances we are expected to overlook (see Prov. 12:16), but a husband's unfaithfulness is far more serious than the annoyance of a neighbor's incessantly barking dog.

I admit that I was actually somewhat relieved to hear her frank admission of these difficult emotions. I assured her that her pain was legitimate, and she didn't need to talk herself out of those tears and that very real outpouring of shame. She needed to continue in the process of forgiving her husband, but she also had to allow herself time for mourning. I said the same thing to her I had suggested to the deacon's wife. "You should wear black as a symbol of mourning the loss. You need to do whatever it takes to grieve the pain you feel right now and be real. Jesus can walk with you through all this."

Why don't we just call it what it is when it hurts so badly? It hurts me even now to think about how we hurt Jesus even more when we don't turn to Him. Jesus "is close to the brokenhearted," and He's right there to heal the brokenhearted as soon as they can admit their hurt to Him.

A Very Personal Example

As we saw in the last chapter, when a person buries his feelings, he also buries the hope of healing, and the fermentation and growth of bitterness begin. *It takes more faith to feel grief than to deny and bury the offense.* Legitimate offense requires genuine forgiveness based on great faith in the Ultimate Forgiver. How ironic that Jesus is referred to as a "rock of offense" (1 Pet. 2:8 KJV), yet His "offense" resulted in His being the ultimate redemption of all offenses.

After I became a believer, I dated a guy in California; he was my first Christian boyfriend. Everyone always said to us, "You are the perfect couple. We can't wait to see how God's going to use you." We worked hand in hand with Youth for Christ, and we traveled and did all these neat things for Jesus. My family moved to Florida during our time of dating, and I stayed in San Diego with a family I knew because my boyfriend had communicated that he and I were going to be a lifelong team.

After a year and a half of dating, he broke up with me. I started crying—not too strange a response for a young woman, wouldn't you say? But his response was "Why are you crying? Where's your faith? You always tell everybody about trusting God—well, why can't you trust God with this right now?"

Whoa! I thought, *Excuse me? Can I recover from the impact of your words first? Now, let me say something to you!*

That's what I would say *today*, but when he used those "Christianese" words on me, the spiritually loaded words that, tragically, people use to manipulate others, I just sputtered out a paraphrase of Romans 8:32 instead: "Oh, that's right, if God spared not His only Son, how much more will He give me all things freely with Him." Still, God had taken what I thought was the best thing that ever came my way, especially from my crazy background: I had a godly man who didn't take advantage of me. But I kept returning to Romans 8:32. I just couldn't wait to see what He was going to give me.

Now to be honest, my response was real. It came from a heart of faith, and Jesus did sustain me. (He eventually gave me the man He had been waiting to surprise me with for all those years. At the time, I had no idea how perfectly God had prepared my husband for me.) But that comment from the guy breaking up with me was all I needed to slam a lid right down on top of all my sadness and humiliation. I had no idea how to feel any of the pain then. So, when anybody called me the next day saying, "Just tell us it's not the truth. You guys haven't broken up, have you?" I responded calmly, "Oh yes, but it's okay because of Romans 8:32." I gave the caller all the verses and spiritualized away my hurts and my heartache.

Yet thank the Lord for one godly man who had the courage to say to me, "You're hurting, aren't you?" This happened weeks later. I looked at him and just burst out crying, the crying I should have done at the beginning. He was the only person who had the nerve to speak to me. Everybody else thought he was very unspiritual, but in fact, he was the fairest person I had ever met, because he was honest about the damage pain does.

Time Doesn't Heal All Wounds

People may say that time heals all wounds, but if someone has not done the hard work of forgiveness, time only moves the pain below the surface. So often a person will say, "It hurts too much to feel the pain again." And my reply is "It hurts more not to feel it." The insidious crime of rape is not what ultimately kills the soul; it is the shaming silence a woman lives with, often for *years*, that holds her hostage to the deep offense. Sexual abuse is a soul-deadening crime not only because of the violent, dishonoring physical treatment but also because of the shame that keeps the victim silent.

A dear friend from college sent me some of her counseling notes years ago:

Deal with incest, abuse, etc., in therapy by:
- Allowing the victims to tell their stories.
- Allowing the victims to grieve.
- Helping victims make new decisions—who they are now, etc.
- Helping them have new experiences.

These notes are so simple and yet so profound. If God's children would just learn to allow the offended to tell their stories and *grieve* the offenses—there would be far less spiritual illness in the body of Jesus. As I said in the last chapter, when pain is buried, it is buried only for a time. When it comes to the surface of one's life, and it *will* come to the surface, it often erupts in destructive behavior that could have been prevented if the person had been able to sufficiently grieve the offense, loss, or devastation. Promiscuity and addiction are common behaviors that erupt from hidden sexual offenses.

While recounting the story of the tragic death of her young son through the carelessness of a surgeon, a dear friend shared with me the agony that rose to the surface during this painful grief process. The toxic heap that erupted resulted in her spouse making bad choices that hurt not only his spiritual life but also the intimacy of his marriage. It is not unusual for a person to make a terrible choice during the pain of tragedy. What is more amazing is that the pain we stuff actually resurrects and intensifies the present pain—enhancing the propensity for an even poorer choice in response.

Shakespeare wisely recommended, "Give sorrow words; the grief that does not speak whispers the o'er-fraught heart and bids it break."

Forgiveness: A Layered Process

God is gracious to us, and there is no question that He does use time to heal—if we cooperate with Him and do the hard work of grieving and forgiving. Sometimes what we cannot see at one stage of our lives becomes crystal clear at another stage. Early in the morning on Christmas Day 1996, Jesus chose to show me hurt that I had buried long before. And it was resurrected so that I could do the hard work of forgiveness.

In the spring of 1973, my future mother-in-law went to her weekly Bible study and asked the group to pray that God would block her son Ken from getting engaged to me. She shared her concern that I was a fraud, that I was a wolf in sheep's clothing, and that her precious son deserved a better helpmate for the ministry he was preparing to enter.

Esther's shaming rejection of me as a potential daughter-in-law was a shocking blow to an already wounded heart. Devastated when I was told what she had done, I went to a beach and wept. The Lord comforted me with 2 Timothy 1:9: "Who hath saved us, and called us with a holy calling, not according to our works, but according to his own purpose and grace, which was given us in Christ Jesus before the world began" (KJV).

With that verse held close to my heart, I was able to face Ken's mom and share with her that God's purpose for me was put in place before the world began, and that neither she nor all the demons of hell could stop His purpose. Can you picture that scene? All that boldness flowing from such a defensive, wounded girl! That verse gave me confidence in God's purpose; yet the healing of my heart did not take place that day. The fact is that I did not genuinely acknowledge all of the deep hurt and anger. To pretend one is not hurt or angry in an attempt to accomplish forgiveness and restore a relationship quickly will only give opportunity for anger to turn into a smoldering bitterness. I moved too quickly past a heart wound.

Now, fast-forward to Christmas morning 1996. I was having my devotions and praying before I joined my family around the Christmas tree. The Lord showed me my heart as a clear, running stream in my life, but then a sudden storm stirred the waters. Floating on top of the water was a rusty, old can I knew represented Esther's rejection of me as "unfit." It had been buried in the mud, and the Holy Spirit used a specific circumstance to shake it free. Realizing how significant this was, I asked the Holy Spirit to resurrect any other rusty cans at the bottom of my heart's stream.

Forgiveness is a layered process, and it wasn't until a full decade later, on December 29, 2006, after a friend challenged me to search my heart for any unforgiveness toward a loved one, that this old wound was revealed again. We talked about how Jesus was assaulted by criticism, slander, and hatred, but He did not allow offense to reside in His heart. That was the heart I desired. So I drove to the beach, and I asked the Lord to reveal any hidden unforgiveness. The Lord brought to my mind an incident that was thirty-three years old. As I looked down the long shoreline, the Lord reminded me of that day in the spring of 1973 when I sat on that very beach crying about Ken's mother rejecting me as "unfit" for her son.

The Lord revealed to me that I had not been mature enough to forgive my mother-in-law at that time in my life. I hadn't even done the hard work of forgiving my abusive father, much less my rejecting future mother-in-law. In that moment, the Lord showed me that I had put on a strong face and moved a raw, painful experience underground, where it fermented for years. Right there on the beach, I began to cry and asked the Lord to forgive me for allowing unforgiveness to have even a moment of residence in my heart. I prayed to be a woman who had an unoffendable heart like Jesus and not someone with a bitter, tough exterior standing guard over her heart wounds.

Honeymoon Warning About Potential Bitterness

While on our honeymoon, my husband and I had the privilege of meeting author Dr. John White. He invited us to have dinner with him, and during dinner Dr. White listened to my life story and kindly warned me, "With so much pain in your past, you will have to be on alert concerning the bitterness that may want to take root even today in your heart. Such a bitter root will harm your precious marriage." His final comment to me was to study thoroughly Hebrews 12:15: "See to it that no one misses the grace of God and that no bitter root grows up to cause trouble and defile many."

You and I need to oversee our hearts on a daily basis. In this crazy world, offense can come daily, and if we don't look to Jesus for the grace to respond appropriately, over time a root of bitterness may find a place in our souls to grow. Bitterness is like an ugly tattoo covering one's skin. So many people are not cognizant of the staining of bitterness all over their faces.

What is particularly frightening about refusing to forgive and enjoying your anger toward someone is that this anger impacts you not only while the offender is alive—when he or she dies, your anger does not subside. The only way to end your anger is to choose to cease sinning and open your heart to forgive—let go—and no longer live in the sorority (fraternity) house of bitterness.

Don't Pledge to the Sorority of Bitterness

Although I never belonged to a sorority in college, I did pledge to a sort of sorority as a young Christian. The commonality joining us as sisters was the root of bitterness, although most of us were clueless about it. Just like anger, bitterness and hostility can be disguised as drivenness, discipline, excessive diligence, and perfectionism. Our disguises convinced us that we had a lot in common—we were women who were not apathetic and wanted to make a difference in the world—especially through overbearing control.

The Lord allowed me to quit this sorority when I was confronted with the unresolved anger that I lived with on a daily basis. So often when my anger was aroused I would deny it and quickly bury it by moving into some project—like cleaning the kitchen floor at midnight because—guess what!—my anger produced insomnia.

When I saw the elaborate root system of my bitterness, I was overwhelmed. How could I possibly deal with so many incidences of hurt and anger? The Lord assured me that by His grace I could "uproot" the bitterness as I willingly faced and confessed my unresolved anger and the many excuses for unforgiveness I had used.

I have now pledged and been accepted into a new club that has male and female members. "A Club for Lovers" is made up of good forgivers who aggressively deal with their anger so that they can freely forgive and be forgiven. Our club motto is "Great Forgiver = Great Lover."

A friend shared his experience with the liberating power of forgiveness:

> *A few years back I was ridiculed, belittled, and (in my eyes) persecuted by a coach. I tried all I could to please this man. But inevitably it was never enough. I felt my confidence and peace begin to slip. I also began to harbor intense bitterness and disdain for this man.*
>
> *Eventually I moved on to another team, but I never let go of the bitterness and my disdain only grew. For two years this continued to be the case, and that is when I was reminded that I am to forgive not because he deserves it but because Christ forgave me. Not only that, but I was to then pray blessings upon this man. The only person I was hurting by not forgiving was me. You see, for two years I experienced an interesting phenomenon. Every game I played I seemed to play in a tunnel—I had no peripheral vision. It was like everything was*

*dark except for maybe twenty yards directly in front of me. I
didn't realize this was even the case until I truly forgave this
coach for the first time in my heart. It was a Saturday night
before a game and the next day when I played in the game it
was as if the lights had been turned back on.*

*The next week God gave me an opportunity to speak with
this coach and ask him to forgive me for not handling things
like Christ. He in turn asked me to forgive him for the things
he had done to me. We now have a relationship in which
we speak by phone every so often. By the way, in the area
of praying blessings upon him, I don't know all of what has
happened in his life but I do know that he has since gone to
the Super Bowl.*

—*Jon Kitna (NFL quarterback)*

Jon's choice to be a good forgiver has splashed over into his
influence as a loving leader among his teammates. He is well on
his way to becoming a Hall of Famer in the Club for Lovers.

Wanting to have an unoffendable heart like Jesus required
that I examine my heart for any area where my love was constrained through shame and unforgiveness. I had the right to
feel sad, betrayed, angry, and resentful when I was publicly
rejected by my future mother-in-law. But I didn't understand or
accept my feelings at that time. I thought a good Christian girl
wouldn't express such anger! But pushing those feelings below
the surface only resulted in their popping up in another place
at another time.

Memories can drench one in shame, but the battle is won
as we drench ourselves in the truths of God's satisfaction with
us. "We're depending on GOD; he's everything we need. What's
more, our hearts brim with joy since we've taken for our own

his holy name. Love us, GOD, with all you've got—that's what we're depending on" (Ps. 33:20–22 THE MESSAGE).

Facing the Feelings

Time does heal, but time heals only the wounds we allow the light of God to shine on and expose. Time ferments and intensifies wounds that are hidden, but God wants us to come to Him with all this pain. Too often we don't face our pain because we are too scared. Sometimes we don't think God will be able to comfort us adequately, but we need to give Him a chance. In truth, He is more than able!

I once counseled a girl at a camp who had just been date-raped. She was in school and had been a virgin. As she told me her story, I started crying and asked her, "What did your dad do when he heard?"

She said, "Oh, my goodness, I couldn't tell anybody, because I know my dad would kill the guy!"

I said, "Wait a minute! You didn't tell your parents because you're trying to protect your father from hurting that boy?" I couldn't believe it, but that's what we train one another to do. We think, *If I tell people, it will be too weighty for them.* That's the way we are about God; we don't always believe He can handle our woes. It's amazing. If He spoke the world into existence, I think He can handle the stress and even the trauma of our lives.

When we do go before our loving Father and face a specific wrong, we also must state the specific feelings caused by the wrong. This is the area where many start faking it. It astounds me when I hear a parent calmly state, "Someone molested my daughter, but I know that God's going to work it out." Believe me, I acknowledge that God can bring good out of bad; I'm proof of it as a survivor of abuse. But who's working with that little girl to go through everything she's feeling? She has real emotions that go with what happened to her body, and these need to be discussed before she can move on. Unfortunately, few want to talk about such feelings.

When Jesus cried in the garden, He wept because He knew He was going to drink the fruit of an unfaithful husband, a father sneaking into a room and molesting a child, and a boy shooting another boy over a girlfriend. He drank all that; He took that on Himself. Why would you think He can't handle it? He wants to walk with us through our hurts. "We have not an high priest which cannot be touched with the feeling of our infirmities" (Heb. 4:15 KJV). Jesus is touched by our suffering. The word *touched* refers to sympathy in "fellow-feeling."[2] He is sympathetic about whatever has hurt you or someone you love. Jesus wants you to admit the pain, and He also wants you to let people talk about *their* pain. Don't keep shutting them down. Walk with them in that pain. Ask hurting people what they're thinking and feeling. Jesus modeled that when He said, "I'm going away, but I'm going to send One who's going to walk with you, the Paraclete" (see John 14:26; 15:26; 16:7, 13). The Holy Ghost is the One who comes right up beside you. He's the best comfort when you're in pain.

When my sister killed herself, I was at a camp preaching to kids about staying pure and saying no to drugs. At the same time, my sister Bobbie was dying from overdosing on eighty quaaludes. That incident caused unimaginable pain for me. I felt the kind of pain where I couldn't breathe, and I hyperventilated in my sleep. During this tragedy I realized, *This is what's going on in the body of Christ.* People are too afraid to admit the pain they've had: the disappointments in their marriages, their children, the families they married into, their dashed dreams. Well, God's big enough for all that. The Cross can take on all that if we will just go to Jesus. And go with one another! Sometimes people are so overwhelmed that you just have to help them go toward Jesus.

Blaming Oneself for the Offense

There is a scene in the Academy Award–winning movie *Good Will Hunting* that perfectly illustrates the damage of self-shame. In the movie, a gifted counselor is working with an unmotivated genius who seems to resist any opportunity for success. The counselor begins to discover the reality of deep abuse that the young man experienced as a child. After the young man again sabotages an incredible opportunity, the counselor—seemingly out of the blue—starts repeating this phrase: "It was not your fault. It was not your fault." Eventually the young man begins to weep. It is very dramatic and very telling. It is clear that this is the first time that message has truly penetrated his elaborate layers of defense and punctured his fuel line of shame. The victim will often blame himself or herself for the abuse and then live buried alive by this insidious shame.

Years ago, a dear friend paid for me to attend a Wounded Heart Conference with Dr. Dan Allender. He is an authority on the subject of the impact of sexual abuse. During the conference, Dr. Allender spoke about Satan's strategic devices, and it was from him that I first heard sexual abuse characterized as a soul-deadening crime. The coffin that one is buried in is the coffin of shame. He quoted the French philosopher

Jean-Paul Sartre, who described shame as the "hemorrhage of the soul."

How to Say Good-bye to Shame

You'll remember the story I told in chapter 1 about revealing the horror of my sexual abuse to a wonderful counselor back when I was in college. But after doing so, I was greatly ashamed that I had told another human being. This rupture of shame caused me to immediately withdraw and return to the emotional underground where I often lived.

Do you remember how I hid this resurrected shame? I pursued Jesus with a passion. I pursued everything with a compelling drive. To a discerning person, this was an obvious manifestation of the wound in my heart that I was breathlessly trying to cover up. Shame is too often the fuel for the overachiever—trying to outrun the heart's damage.

And how did God respond to my going undercover? Years later, He used my two precious children to escort me back into professional counseling. Deep in my heart I knew that whatever I did not resolve emotionally, I would reproduce in my children. Children often carry our pain. You see, He allows the pain to lie low when He knows that you're not willing to look at it. The resistance from the shamed heart cries, *I didn't sign up for this! I didn't ask to be abused! I didn't even choose this, so why do I have to think about it?* Quite honestly, counseling felt to me like a revictimization, so I stopped for a few years.

Well, God is so loving that He will give you someone who can really walk through it with you. God gave me a woman who heard me speak and who said, "Would you come to my office and tell me your story?" So I said, "You mean my testimony?

Sure!" But her response was, "No, Jackie, I do want to hear your testimony, but I want to hear about what made you this passionate. My sense is that something dark passed over your life."

I was stunned that it was so obvious! But she had dealt with sexual abuse, so she recognized the signs. She took me through a book by Dr. Eliana Gil called *Outgrowing the Pain*, and until I read that little book, I didn't realize how much of who I was hid my damage. I thought I was just an outgoing, driven student because I was bright. What I had not seen until that time was that I was fueled by fear that someone might find out that I was damaged goods. You see, it was that fuel line of shame propelling my driven nature. What I learned from the book was that some part of my personality was certainly what I was born with, but events in my childhood determined the intensity and the direction of my personality. I became more aggressive because I didn't want anybody to find out how terrified and damaged I was inside.

So often a woman will confide her deep heart wounds to me, and the next time I see her, I can tell if she has retreated back into shame. If she avoids me, I know that she was honest, but shame beat her up about sharing her secret struggles. The enemy uses shame to keep God's kids in prison.

Boldly Bid Shame Good-bye

Why is it so hard for a Christian to say good-bye to shame? For too many Christians, shame is like an enemy outpost. Lewis Smedes gave this definition: "Shame is a vague, undefined heaviness that presses on our spirit, dampens our gratitude for the goodness of life, and slackens the free flow of joy."[3]

Although we as Christians know that Jesus died to pay for

our sins, we are constantly assaulted by Satan's favorite tool. "Shame on you," people say. As forgiven believers, we know that there is *no condemnation* in Christ (see Rom. 8:1), but still we struggle.

Last night at church, the worship leader read a passage of Scripture that floored me! The passage was Luke 7:36–50. In my Bible (NIV) the passage has a subtitle: "Jesus Anointed by a Sinful Woman." This sinful woman (notorious in her town) walked into a most condemning situation—the home of Simon the Pharisee. It would be like a prostitute showing up for a covered-dish dinner at the pastor's house! But this sinful woman did not allow condemning shame to keep her from anointing and kissing the feet of the Holy One of Israel.

Now, how did a *sinful* woman walk past a judgmental, self-righteous man like Simon? Here's how: she was so focused on Jesus Christ that she was not tripped up by a Shaming Simon! This sinful woman did something so radical, so passionate, that her single-minded focus on Jesus kept her from being frozen in her steps by shame's chilly finger of condemnation.

Satan daily uses the judgmental Shaming Simons of this world to accuse, confuse, and trip up God's less-than-perfect children. When a believer focuses on Jesus, the Shaming Simons of this world have no influence. On the other hand, when a struggling believer focuses on the comments of a Shaming Simon, she is stopped in her tracks before she ever gets to the feet of Jesus.

Again, we are to come "boldly" unto the throne of grace (Heb. 4:16 KJV), and we must resist the Shaming Simons who continually whisper how "unworthy" we are. We need to focus on the forgiving Savior rather than the judgmental Simons. In doing this, we may boldly say good-bye to shame.

Do you know how God views our failures, the very things for which we fear others' judgments? He expects them. He forgives them. He uses them. Here are two great verses to memorize that will break the pointing finger of any Shaming Simon:

Do not be afraid; you will not suffer shame. Do not fear disgrace; you will not be humiliated. *You will forget the shame of your youth.* (Isa. 54:4, emphasis added)

Instead of their shame my people will receive a double portion, and instead of disgrace they will rejoice in their inheritance; and so they will inherit a double portion in their land, and everlasting joy will be theirs. (Isa. 61:7)

The enemy of our souls does not want us to be delivered from our unhealthy shame. We need to toss a grenade of truth (see John 8:32) into this enemy outpost of unhealthy shame that exists in our hearts and minds.

You will probably encounter a Shaming Simon in the days ahead, so stay focused on Jesus and be ready to forgive this blind person. The next time you get ready to kiss the feet of Jesus in worship, don't be surprised if you hear a Shaming Simon groaning in the background.

A. W. Tozer wisely said:

So, it becomes the devil's business to keep the Christian's spirit imprisoned. He knows that the believing and justified Christian has been raised up out of the grave of his sins and trespasses. From that point on, Satan works that much harder to keep us bound and gagged, actually imprisoned in our grave clothes. He knows that if we continue in this kind of bondage...we are not much better than when we were spiritually dead.[4]

Recently, I received a phone call from a very upset friend because her husband had overreacted to one of her comments. When she shared her comment with me, one thing came to mind—shame. Her comment was completely innocent to anyone who isn't filled with shame. I told her that the residue of shame that still exists in her husband's heart has skewed his understanding, so he doesn't hear clearly her suggestions or simple criticisms. Critics are a terror to a person with unhealthy shame!

For years my own husband has expressed how puzzled he is when I become so defensive about the slightest criticism. Only in the last decade have we come to understand the impact of shame on my heart. If you find yourself overreacting to a suggestion or constructive criticism, ask the Lord to show you whether or not your reaction is based on pride or unhealthy shame. "I can answer those who taunt me, for I trust in your word" (Ps. 119:42 NLT).

Slam Dunk Against Shame

I read this story seventeen years ago. It is a profound illustration of the power of shame to keep us hostage to past wounds. But more important, it is an illustration of the only sure way of release. Here is "Geri's Story":

> I had stopped to call on Geri, a young mother with a serious alcohol problem. As I walked to the door, the Holy Spirit said to me, "Get Geri to talk to Me." After exchanging social pleasantries with Geri and her husband, I said, "Geri, God wants you to talk to Him." I told her how simply we may hear God and she asked the Father, "Would You please tell me what You think of me?" His reply to her was, "You are worth a lot more than you think you are."

I said, "Ask Him what you are worth." She did, and then said, "I don't understand the answer. He said, 'Geri, you are worth as much as I am.'"

For a moment I was perplexed too, and then I saw it. Worth is often determined by the price paid for something. Christ gave His life for us so we could have life. Life for life. His life for my life.[5]

Geri's destructive choices with alcohol created a damaged-goods mentality. It is so common for those with heart wounds to further harm themselves through the bondage of shame. A person who won't forgive another for a deep heart wound actually harms herself through a life of shamed captivity.

But seeing ourselves as having great worth to God—as Geri heard, "You are worth as much as I am"—will allow us not only to leave the prison of shame and but also to forgive freely. People who understand the enormity of the price paid to forgive them will grasp that the only unforgivable sin is the one they won't forgive.

Henri Nouwen once said, "The greatest danger in the spiritual life is not success or popularity or power—it's self-rejection."[6] The danger of allowing unforgiveness to maintain residency in our hearts is that shame will continue to belittle the vessel in which it is reigning. "May my accusers perish in shame; may those who want to harm me be covered with scorn and disgrace" (Ps. 71:13). Instead, I want to be covered with the mercy that empowers me to forgive—and love—freely.

When we bid shame good-bye, we can begin the courageous consideration of all the other hesitations in our hearts that keep us from forgiving our offenders. Let's look next at the common hesitations and excuses that keep so many people held hostage to yesterday.

MAKE IT PERSONAL

1. Are you surprised by the suggestion that shame develops when hurt is hidden? If so, share what you thought produced shame in a heart (see Ps. 34:5).

2. "Wounds that are hidden only erode self-esteem through the screaming message of dishonoring shame." Do you suspect you have hidden wounds? If so, what will you do about them? (See Isa. 54:4.)

3. "Shame allows the past to trample the present with muddy footprints." Has this happened to you or someone you love? Describe the situation.

4. Have you assumed that time heals all wounds? What do you think about the fermentation of a wound that is hidden? Do you have any long-fermenting hurts? Have you shared them with anyone yet?

5. Discuss how a rush to forgive denies the hurt experienced. Have you ever seen this happen? What was the result in the person who rushed to forgive?

6. How is the layered process of forgiveness similar to the process of grief?

7. Describe the bitterness that takes root when the forgiveness process is not completed. Have you experienced this? (See Heb. 12:15.)

8. Have you experienced the freedom of saying good-bye to shame? If so, can you share a little of the context? (See Isa. 61:7.)

Part II

Excuses for Remaining a Hostage to Yesterday

Chapter 3

Authentic Forgiveness

How often have you considered that one of the first remarks made by our risen Lord had to do with forgiveness? Jesus spoke of peace, receiving the Holy Spirit, and forgiveness that had just been made forever possible because of His death on the cross. "Jesus said, 'Peace be with you! As the Father has sent me, I am sending you.' And with that he breathed on them and said, 'Receive the Holy Spirit. If you forgive anyone his sins, they are forgiven; if you do not forgive them, they are not forgiven'" (John 20:21–23). Jesus knew that it would take the power of the Holy Spirit for a human being to do something as superhuman as forgive. Yet, as we have seen, even with the Holy Spirit we resist the process of forgiving—sometimes without even realizing it! Not only can we be bound up by lies and crippled by shame, we can remain hostage to unforgiveness with a whole assortment of excuses at hand. That will be the focus of the next chapters, the six classic excuses I have taught about for many years. But before I launch into them, let's get clear on what it is that we are resisting. What does it mean to forgive, and why should we work at it?

In its most simple form, to forgive is to recognize that you have been hurt or offended, to bring the resulting hurt, anger, shock, or sadness to God, and then, by faith, to declare forgiveness. In our Christian walk, we learn to walk by faith, not by sight; I'm proposing that we forgive by faith and not by sight. Then we do it again, and again. Shampoo, rinse, repeat.

I'll go into that repeating part later, but I can't emphasize enough that one of the great misconceptions about forgiveness is that it is a onetime act. The only surefire, onetime act of forgiveness was that of Jesus Christ on the cross!

When you take the seven-letter word *forgive* and break it apart, the meaning is profound:

For: a preposition—on behalf of, having a reason
Give: freely transfer possession[1]

Now consider these meanings together. On behalf of the Cross and Jesus, I freely transfer the possession of the capacity to forgive. Or, the other definition of the preposition *for* is "having a reason." Now, that has a strong implication when you add Jesus or the Cross—then you have the greatest reason to forgive. And this freely transferred possession of loving forgiveness exists entirely because of the cross of Jesus. Because of Calvary, forgiveness should be a familiar habit for Christians. Remember? Paul told us to be "forgiving [of] each other, just as in Christ God forgave you" (Eph. 4:32).

Remember this: we are most like Jesus not when we are perfect, but when we are forgiving. We were purchased with the scars of Jesus, and by His scars will ours be healed. This reality is profoundly expressed in a story I read about Julian of Norwich (the popular English mystic, 1342–1416). When Julian was thirty years old, she was taken seriously ill, and when it seemed as if she would die, a priest laid a crucifix on her face and whispered, "Open your eyes and look into the face of the One who understands the depth of your suffering."[2]

When I read that comment, I burst into tears. I realized that Julian looked into the face of the One who gives *me* the strength to forgive—even the unforgivable. Because of this One who understands the depth of our suffering through offenses and because of the corresponding capacity of forgiving grace, the Christian is left with no other option than to forgive.

After reading this story, I had a brainstorm. I thought about purchasing a good-sized cross and carrying it in my backpack to the conferences I do each weekend. Whenever I counseled someone struggling with unforgiveness, I would ask her to close her eyes, and I would hold the cross before her face. Then I would instruct her to open her eyes, look at the symbol of the passion of the Christ, and realize anew that there is only one option for the forgiven ones—to forgive.

First John says, "You say you love God, whom you can't see, but you can't love your brother, whom you do see" (see 4:20). Do you see the problem, the paradox there? When Christians do not grasp how much they have been forgiven, a level of pride blinds them to this fact: before they were born again, they were actually enemies of God: "If, when we were God's enemies, we were reconciled to him through the death of his Son, how much more, having been reconciled, shall we be saved through his life!" (Rom. 5:10).

This connection was captured in an earth-shattering comment written by a theologian named Miroslav Volf, whose daughter was raped and killed by an attacking army: "One cannot ultimately understand forgiveness until we recognize that we were once enemies who were invited into the forgiving embrace of the eternal Triune God, through the open arms of the crucified Christ."[3]

When one has experienced the loving embrace of God, forgiving is the inevitable response...even if a man is forgiving those who raped and murdered his precious daughter.

The Art of Forgiving

As Christians, we must remember that we have been forgiven for so much, and yet it seems we are often the worst forgivers around. We should be the best, leading the world by example! To do that, we have to practice.

The heart of emotional health is the ability to forgive. Good relationships (marriages, parent/child, and friendships) are made up of those who have learned how to forgive. So many relational crimes are committed and so many relationships end because people have not learned the *art* of forgiving. When one thinks of *art*, one can't help but think of terms like *creativity* and *imaginative skill*. Forgiving is a specific skill that actually utilizes more creativity than one would have ever imagined. This book will touch on many creative responses that the Bible suggests for those who want to be skilled in the art of forgiving.

Forgiveness, like painting or sculpting, takes practice. With art, one starts with a small project and then moves to more complex and imaginative expression. With forgiving, you need to start with small hurts (marginal offenses) and work your way up to the big ones (mortal offenses). Let's get a better understanding of what I mean here.

Offenses: Marginal and Mortal

Mortal offenses are those inflicted upon us. They are indis- putable injuries that have been perpetrated against us like abuse, betrayal, or abandonment. By comparison, a marginal offense is often the result of merely being in the presence of a flawed human being who offends simply because he or she is breathing—you know, everyday rudeness, sarcasm, and self- ishness. The Greek word for "offense" (*proskomma*) means "an obstacle to stub on, trip one up, dash one's foot against."[4] When you read "to stub on," can't you just feel the jolt of walking along and suddenly stubbing your toe? It is a genuine hurt, most of the time not life-altering, but it still hurts. Marginal offenses are like that stubbed toe. They sure smart, but they don't have to be life-altering, especially with the application of a grace- saturated attitude of forgiving freely.

People can define their hurts in many different ways. One person responds to a sarcastic comment as if she were punched in the gut, and another person shrugs off a pattern of scath- ing verbal abuse as just an annoyance. Here's an interesting example. I recounted an experience I had had as a young child to a friend of mine, calling it a marginal offense. Her definition did not exactly line up with mine! See what you think.

One day as my class began taking a test, a kid behind me tapped my shoulder and asked to borrow a pencil. I whispered, "We're not supposed to speak during the test." Well, the sister heard me and told me to come to the front of the class immedi- ately! She asked all the students to put their pencils down. She pulled her chair from behind her desk, placed it in front of the class, sat down on the chair, and then asked me to come and sit on her lap. After I was situated, the nun said, "Now, class, we are going to sing, 'Rock-a-Bye-Baby' to Jackie, because only a baby doesn't know how to follow directions when she is told." The kids and the sister began to sing, and I just cried softly.

In a quickly returned e-mail, here is what my friend wrote: "To my mind, this is much farther along the continuum towards mortal than marginal." She was horrified by the nun's behavior and called it abusive. A marginal offense is when your neighbor snaps at you; a mortal offense is pouring shame over someone.

For me, the "singing nun" experience seemed like a marginal offense when compared to the mortal offense of sexual abuse. But my friend's response highlights the different perceptions people have about being offended. Marginal offenses can sometimes be minimized in relation to much deeper offenses; but ironically, they can also become exaggerated in perception because of a mortal offense that created a heart wound that is not yet healed. No matter how one experiences them, marginal offenses are still emotional storms that break a few tree branches in our internal landscape.

The art, the skill, of forgiving is mandatory for successfully maneuvering through both marginal and mortal offenses. Jesus gave us a hint about why this is necessary in the great chapter on forgiveness, Matthew 18. There Jesus made a remark that is often missed by even the most observant reader (including me), but a friend drew my attention to this passage of Scripture—showing that even after forty years of studying God's Word, for me it is "new every morning." Verse 7 says, "Woe unto the world because of offenses! For it must needs be that offenses come" (KJV).

Here Jesus stated that being offended is *inevitable* while journeying through this life, and becoming a great forgiver is the best training for handling those inevitable offenses. It is so amazing to study some of the words in the Greek for "offense." They always refer to stumbling, being tripped up, and being trapped. I can't help but consider the trap of unforgiveness. Note the progression there! When I am offended, I am first *trapped* by the rude remark, and then I am *imprisoned* through unforgiveness. Forgiveness is the key to my release.

Forgiveness Is Always a Gift!

For two decades I have traveled throughout the United States carrying a collection of gift bags in my suitcase. People have called me the "spiritual bag lady." Everywhere I go to speak, I always speak on forgiveness. So what do *gift bags* have to do with forgiveness? I use them as a visual to remind the audience that *forgiveness is always a gift.*

In this collection, I have little bags and big bags, because offense comes in all sizes. In fact, I have one *very* large bag that represents the deepest heart wounds—like rape, incest, divorce, or murder. Forgiveness, after all, is required in different proportions that correspond to the offense or harm or hurt.

My response to an offense determines my future, so I often visualize a gift bag with a specific person's name on it. The offense was specific, and the offender has a name. I see this gift bag as something that I prepare to give by faith, and when I have given this gift (figuratively, not literally), I have by faith become a "cheerful giver." Of course such a gift-giving experience requires faith in God's grace to behave myself.

How do we get such strength to act properly even when offended? In the little book of James, a powerful statement is made: "God resists the proud, but gives grace to the humble" (4:6 NKJV). In this passage, the "humble" are those knocked down by a circumstance. God gives grace to people who have been knocked down by someone. How many times have harsh words knocked you to the ground? Maybe you didn't fall down physically, but internally you were slammed right to the ground. So many times when people make remarks that are really damaging, they are absolutely clueless. My best friend and I have a description for such people: "They have no filter."

Nevertheless, whether people are intentional or clueless with their harsh, demeaning comments, there is grace to get back up and into the battle of life. In fact, I envision this gigantic warehouse where God stores a bounty of gorgeously wrapped packages of grace just waiting to be delivered to those who are knocked down but not knocked out. God's delivery package can energize one to stand in confidence rather than retire from the human race to avoid another heart wound. And when we receive His grace package, we have just the thing to put into our gift bags of forgiveness.

As I described, these bags come in all shapes and sizes, because authentic forgiveness addresses offenses of all shapes and sizes. The grace to forgive applies to the whole spectrum of offenses, from the marginal to the mortal—forgiving the unimaginable.

When I was in ninth grade, my mom and I were discussing my being invited to a party by a particularly cute guy, and I mentioned my surprise that he invited me and not my best friend, Judy. My mom replied, "You aren't as pretty as Judy, but you have a great personality that will get you dates when your looks won't." Now, my mom did not intend to hurt my feelings, but that marginal offense followed me for years, making it very hard for me to ever accept any compliment about my looks.

Certainly such marginal offenses operate in our church communities as well. While writing this book, I received an e-mail from a woman who had been offended by another Christian woman. Here is the response I sent to her:

> *Precious sister, I have some great news for you. While research-*
> *ing every word translated "forgiveness" in God's Word, one of the*
> *words I found was... ready for this? In Genesis 50:17, the Hebrew*
> *idiom for "forgiveness" means: "lifting up the head."[5] Because of*
> *Jesus, you have the ability to lift your head and walk upright with*
> *confidence. You can attend the women's event where the offending*
> *woman will be. You can forgive her in advance, and you can raise*
> *your head and walk in with God's confidence. If you, by faith,*
> *forgive this offensive woman, you can see the offender face-to-face*
> *and remain upright, full of God's love rather than anger.*
>
> *Remember, to forgive means to let go of what you want from*
> *this woman. Don't rent space to that hurt any longer! You*
> *need to move out of the condo of victimization and into the*
> *mansion of the unoffendable heart of Jesus. This is something*
> *you do by faith and not by feelings. One of the reasons we*
> *remain stuck is our pride. That pride is fueled by our shock*
> *that a fellow Christian would act so unkindly toward us.*
>
> *Raise your head, go to this event, and receive further*
> *blessings because you forgave this woman. On the way to the*
> *event, ask God's forgiveness for considering letting this woman*
> *control you more than God!*

I wonder how many people decide against going to church, a Bible study group, or an event because they can't stomach the prospect of seeing a particular person. They can't comprehend lifting up their heads by forgiving. How sad to consider the control that others have over our attending various events that would feed our souls. We miss the meal over the "gag reflex" of anticipating someone who offended or hurt us.

It may be that at this point you are thinking, *Of course I can forgive or learn to forgive things like this.* But here is the clincher. There comes a point for all of us where we say—in our minds, by our actions, in our hearts—"No way, *not that!*" It's at that line, the one we have drawn in the sand, where our resistance, hesitations, and excuses kick in. At that line, we screech to a halt, dig in our heels, and excuse ourselves from forgiving. In essence, we also stop ourselves from loving. In the next chapters, we will look at the excuses we use to remain unforgiving—and ultimately unloving.

MAKE IT PERSONAL

1. Do you find yourself doubting that Jesus truly understands the depth of your suffering? If yes, explain.

2. Do you see yourself as a good forgiver? Why or why not? How can you become a better forgiver? (See John 20:21–23; Eph. 4:32.)

3. "The heart of emotional health is the ability to forgive." Do you believe this? Why? Have you ever seen it in action?

4. Are you frustrated with the inevitability of offenses being committed against you and those you love? Do you think a person can avoid being offended? If so, how? (See Matt. 18:7 KJV.)

5. Discuss the difference between "marginal" and "mortal" offenses. Do you think the difference is always clear? Share a marginal offense you have forgiven recently. Then, if you will, share a mortal offense that you are still struggling to forgive.

6. When you've been offended, have you avoided people? What effect did this have? (See 1 John 4:20.)

Chapter 4

Held Hostage by the Size of the Offense

In this chapter we'll begin to examine, one by one, the six most commonly used excuses for not forgiving our offenders:

1. The offense was too great.
2. The memories of the offense are so vivid.
3. The offense was repeated.
4. You want to make the person pay for the offense.
5. You are too angry to even consider forgiving this person.
6. The offender didn't say, "I am sorry."

The Offense Was Too Great

Everybody has experienced or can imagine an offense "too big to forgive." I would like to share a story with you that may put things into perspective.

When I read the following story, I decided that Susanne Geske was a great demonstration of the reality that forgiveness is always a gift. To my mind, her example silences all the hesitations to forgive that I will address in this book.

On April 18, 2007, three Christians were murdered in Turkey. They included a German missionary named Tilmann Geske, a missions worker from Turkey; Necati Aydin, a Turkish pastor; and Ugur Yuksel, who had recently converted from Islam. According to *Christianity Today*, "Young radicals feigning curiosity about Christianity" tied up the men and stabbed them again and again, finally cutting their throats. Later Susanne Geske (Tilmann's widow) "made a strong impression on the Turkish public by forgiving her husband's attackers as she spoke on national television."[1]

Perhaps Susanne's experience seems surreal. Well, here is another example of a woman claiming her ability to forgive in a scenario that might be *more* imaginable, yet no easier to forgive. "Eve's" husband was caught in a compromising relationship with one of his male students. This woman was asked if she was going to divorce him, and her response absolutely shocked me as a newlywed when I heard the story: "This is not grounds for divorce, but grounds for forgiveness."

Whether you face forgiving the unforgivable as Susanne has or forgiving someone's rude treatment of you—forgiveness is always a gift. Forgiving someone you love is difficult enough—it's especially difficult having to forgive someone you don't even like! Jesus said, "If you love those who love you, what reward will you get? Are not even the tax collectors doing that?" (Matt. 5:46).

When you are hesitating to forgive, it would be helpful to reread Matthew 18. The parable in this chapter reflects Jesus' heart reply to our hesitation to forgive the unforgivable. You know, the most unforgivable sin is the one you won't forgive. Jesus paid it all when He cried out, "It is finished!" His blood can permeate every Grand Canyon of sin and offense. Here is Jesus' heart in a story:

> The kingdom of heaven is like a king who wanted to settle accounts with his servants. As he began the settlement, a man who owed him ten thousand talents was brought to him. Since he was not able to pay, the master ordered that he and his wife and his children and all that he had be sold to repay the debt. The servant fell on his knees before him. "Be patient with me," he begged, "and I will pay back everything." The servant's master took pity on him, canceled the debt and let him go.
>
> But when that servant went out, he found one of his fellow servants who owed him a hundred denarii. He grabbed him and began to choke him. "Pay back what you owe me!" he demanded. His fellow servant fell to his knees and begged him, "Be patient with me, and I will pay you back." But he refused. Instead, he went off and had the man thrown into prison until he could pay the debt. When the other servants saw what had happened, they were greatly distressed and went and told their master everything that had happened. Then the master called the servant in. "You wicked servant," he said, "I canceled all that debt of yours because you begged me to. Shouldn't you have had mercy on your fellow servant just as I had on you?"
>
> In anger his master turned him over to the jailers to be tortured, until he should pay back all he owed. This is how my heavenly Father will treat each of you unless you forgive your brother from your heart. (Matt. 18:23–35)

In this passage it is easy to assume that the greatest offense was the debt of ten thousand talents. I have heard so many different amounts for the debt—some have said it was like a million dollars in our day. Jesus tells another parable where there is a distribution of one, five, and ten talents. So when I consider that a man owed the king ten thousand talents, it must have been a big debt!

This man threw himself down before the master, begging for mercy as the punishment was being announced: "The master ordered that he and his wife and his children and all that he had be sold to repay the debt" (v. 25). I can only imagine how loudly this man was pleading for mercy when suddenly he thought he heard the unthinkable! *Am I dreaming, or did I just hear my master cancel my debt?* The master indeed had said, "I forgive you, the debt is canceled." If the story ended here, we would have a glimpse of mercy bestowed and a debt canceled. But the power-punching part of this illustration is yet to come.

Well, the servant was leaving, and he wasn't completely out of the palace before he ran into a fellow servant: "When that servant went out, he found one of his fellow servants who owed him a hundred denarii" (v. 28). Now, one hundred denarii is just a few dollars. What was this man's immediate response to a debt he was owed? He began to choke his fellow servant! If you've just been forgiven a million-dollar debt and you run into someone who owes you ten dollars, shouldn't your spontaneous reply be, "You don't owe me anything, brother! Go, and be at peace"? Here was a servant who was just forgiven a great debt, but his response to a minor or marginal debt was to start choking the one who owed him.

While the ungrateful servant had the fellow servant in a choke hold, another who witnessed this unforgiving behavior immediately reported it to the master. And, of course, when the master heard about this unforgiving behavior, he was angry.

"'You wicked servant,' he said, 'I canceled all that debt of yours because you begged me to. Shouldn't you have had mercy on your fellow servant just as I had on you?'" (vv. 32–33).

Notice that Jesus used the term *wicked* to describe this unforgiving behavior. How many times have you heard a Christian describe unforgiveness as "wicked behavior"? A desire to avoid wickedness should be enough to inspire us to reconsider our resistance to forgive an offense that seems unforgivable. If that is not enough inspiration for you, then consider what Jesus said in verses 34–35: "In anger his master turned him over to the jailers to be tortured, until he should pay back all he owed. This is how my heavenly Father will treat each of you unless you forgive your brother from your heart."

The master is angry about the stingy unforgiveness of the most blessed servant, but Jesus' comparative reference to the heavenly Father's displeasure with unforgiving behavior is what's truly sobering. As I consider that, I will tell you this: I don't want to be on the wrong side of the Master's anger.

All who are followers of Jesus have, like this servant, been forgiven an enormous debt. I don't know the numerical equation for the highest number imaginable, but I do know that the debt Jesus paid with His precious blood places each of us right in this parable with the servant forgiven an unimaginable debt. Few of us realize just how much we've been forgiven, and that is likely why we are not as forgiving as Jesus desires us to be. We have been freely forgiven so that we can freely forgive others. We are to be forgiving not because someone deserves it, but as a response to having been forgiven. Too many people wait for someone to earn forgiveness, but that's not forgiveness—that's a wage, not a gift. Jesus calls it the gift of God, and He bestowed it on a desperate group that sorely needed it.

Forgiveness is a gift you give not only to the offender but to yourself. In Luke 6:37, "Forgive, and ye shall be forgiven" (KJV), the Greek word translated "forgiveness" is *apoluno*. Its definition is thrilling to me: "free fully, relieve, dismiss, let die, pardon, divorce, loose, and set at liberty."[2]

As I looked through this list, I loved the first phrase: "free fully." This freedom is not only about the offender but about me, the offended. Forgiving is the releasing of *me*, my liberation in the truest sense. To forgive liberates me to continue to grow and thrive in my intimate relationship with Jesus Christ, to do God's will without tripping over a trap of bitterness. When I refuse to be "divorced" from suffocating unforgiveness, I am trapped in bitterness toward the offender. But when I, by faith, dismiss, divorce, and set at liberty my focus on the offender's behavior—I discover that the one "set at liberty," the one "freed fully," is the one who is forgiving—not the one forgiven. When I let people "off the hook," they are then placed on God's hook, and He alone knows best what to do in relation to the offender (see Prov. 3:12).

People sometimes live so long with offense in their hearts they assume it is just part of who they are. They don't even realize they need to give themselves this gift of liberty. But years of harboring unforgiveness have a profound effect on people (I will address that more in future chapters).

I want you to have a chance to purge your heart of unwanted offense and unforgiveness. My hope is that you will cathartically rid yourself of the toxic by-products of lingering offense in your heart—unwanted feelings, memories, and heart grief—which have long been covered over by behaviors attempting to disguise those wounds. Learning to forgive is not only a spiritual purging, it is also an opportunity to remove the mask you have worn for too many years—and possibly didn't even know you had on.

The Flushing Brigade

I have been gathering stories about people forgiving others for various offenses, and I received one that made me laugh, then turned out to be an incredible idea. Here is the e-mail behind the inspiration of the "flushing brigade": "You should ask my husband about the time he went to speak and realized he couldn't because he was struggling with unforgiveness. He went into the bathroom at the church, wrote the names of those he hadn't forgiven on toilet paper, and flushed them down the toilet! He told the Lord that was an outward expression of his inward desire to forgive and let go! Pretty cool, huh?!"

At a women's retreat where I was teaching, we discussed the issue of forgiving the offender. When the question-and-answer session was finished, a woman came up and shared the story of being raped at the age of thirteen by four men and the impact that crime has had on her life. This wounded woman asked me to pray about doing some kind of specific forgiveness ritual for herself and the many hurting women at the retreat. I told her I would pray. As I was going to my room, the e-mail about "flushing" the offenders' names came to my mind, and I knew that was the thing to do!

That night, I walked to the platform with a roll of toilet paper in my hand and told the audience I would be waiting in the lobby for any woman who was struggling to forgive. I'm sure that image confused a few people! But then I explained that a common word used for "forgiveness" is *aphiemi*, which means "to send away."[3] So our "flushing brigade" was going to symbolically send away the offenders' names. Some seventy-five women joined me, and I gleefully passed out pieces of toilet paper. Women began to write names on them. When everyone was ready, the group split up between two bathrooms, and the flushing began!

That night, while we may have overwhelmed the conference center's plumbing, we also had a great experience of cathartic release—complete with plenty of laughter—right into the Texas sewer system!

The Gift Cannot Be Given
Without the Fuel of Faith

When we refuse to forgive because, we reason, "the offense was too great," we are operating on a false belief that to remain angry or in self-pity is a form of self-protection. Behind this hesitation is the ultimate reason for our unforgiveness: our lack of faith. If you're having a hard time with some of this material, it may be because your faith right now is a little shaky. But consider this: you can forgive as effectively as your faith is strong.

It takes faith to obey God in what He has instructed us to do with respect to forgiveness. How ironic that we begin our journey of faith by receiving forgiveness for our sins and yet totally miss that the whole journey of faith is a chance to forgive others by faith, just as we were so freely forgiven. A Hebrew word refers to one's readiness to forgive: *sallah*. It is found in Psalm 86:5, which declares that God is *sallah*—which means "ready to forgive."[4]

You may be thinking, *Of course God is ready to forgive. He is God. He is capable of forgiving completely. But I am a mere human even on my best day!* In our humanness, such an assignment may often seem disproportionate to our faith's capacity.

In order to grow in our capacity to forgive, we need to grow in our knowledge of and confidence in God's Word. "Faith comes by hearing, and hearing by the word of God" (Rom. 10:17 NKJV). When I was a new Christian, my capacity to forgive by faith was very small. But as I grew in my knowledge of God's heart in print (His Word), I grew in my faith to forgive.

As you know, I grew up in a home that required a sizable capacity to forgive. To forgive my father for being so abusive and to forgive my mother for staying with such a harmful man took years of growth in my faith. My readiness to forgive grew as my confidence grew in *El Elyon*, the Most High God.

Whenever you are struggling to forgive, here is a verse to whisper to yourself: "You are my strength; come quickly to my aid!" (Ps. 22:19 NLT). Jesus will give you the strength to forgive by faith—not by feelings, but by your will, which is standing firm on your faith. Remember, forgiveness is an issue of obedience, not of following your feelings. And faith alone can move you toward obedience in spite of whatever feelings you have.

Furthermore, ask God to teach you and to increase your faith. Ask Him to help you become more consistent in His Word so you can become a good forgiver. That way, the next time your mother-in-law makes a comment or your sister says something offensive, you can think, *I'm choosing to forgive you right now so that you don't control me, but Jesus does.* Because I will tell you again, those you have not forgiven are controlling you right now; they are the ones who are on the throne of your life, not Jesus.

Angry unforgiveness does not always manifest itself fatally.

Author David Seamands told a story at a Healing of Memories Conference in 1992 that profoundly illustrated the danger of shoving one's unforgiving anger deep in the heart. He was counseling a young woman who had been abused by her dad. After weeks of listening compassionately to her stories, he said, "Are you ready?" And she asked, "For what?" He said, "You need to kneel here in my office and you need, by faith, to forgive your dad." Her response was, "You're crazy! I would never forgive him." Dr. Seamands persisted, "No, you don't understand. If you don't forgive by faith and let this thing go, it will control you forever." She left his office very angry and never returned.

Seventeen years later, according to Dr. Seamands, she disclosed that she had since been through divorce and a nervous breakdown. Then she said, "I should have knelt with you and forgiven him, because it has controlled me all these years."

Faith is fuel for forgiveness. They are inextricably linked. Jesus was the ultimate demonstration of faith in the Father, and this faith allowed Him to forgive freely the blasphemous accusations from the Pharisees before going to the cross (see John 7:20), to forgive while suffering on the cross (see Luke 23:24), and to forgive every day since the Cross (see 1 John 1:9; 2:1).

Forgiveness and Reconciliation

Before we move to the next chapter, I want to clarify the difference between forgiveness and reconciliation. Forgiveness I can give freely. I can let go of the offense, flush it away, and find release. I can do this by faith, regardless of what the other person does. Reconciliation, on the other hand, comes through an act of God touching the heart of the offender, and the offender, in turn, coming and asking the offended for forgiveness. Let me give an example.

I forgave my father for his verbal and sexual abuse, but my father never acknowledged to God or to me the offenses he committed. The reconciliation between my father and me never occurred, and he has died. *However*, I lived out forgiveness by praying and loving (with healthy boundaries) my dad until the day he died.

I can *forgive* people who have never repented by letting go and no longer being preoccupied with their offense or their lack of repentance. *Reconciliation* involves their repentance—and that is a God-sized event! People confuse reconciliation with forgiveness. But let's keep them untangled. Remember the definition highlighted earlier: forgiving is a gift I give because of Jesus' gift to me. It is a gift I bestow upon my offender and a gift I give to myself. Forgiveness is also a gift I give to God. Such a response in faith and obedience is, indeed, an offering to God. Reconciliation is the gift exchanged *between* me and the offender when he or she has repented. Because I have already forgiven, I am not held hostage to that person's offensive behavior, waiting for him or her to repent. Forgiveness is my being set free, and reconciliation is when the relationship between me and the offender is healed, but that healing is up to God, not us.

Relationships, after all, are what forgiveness is all about. God wants us to have sustained and empathetic relationships. We can do this only by freely forgiving and freely loving. God alone can open the heart of the offender, not only to acknowledge the offensive behavior but also to make amends. Making amends often requires an occasion of asking forgiveness.

MAKE IT PERSONAL

1. Describe an offense you find "unforgivable." Does God agree that it is "unforgivable"? How do you know? (See Matt. 18:23–35.)
2. What do you think about Susanne Geske's forgiving response to the murderous mutilation of her husband by three young men? Does her story inspire you somehow?
3. Discuss the difference between forgiveness and reconciliation. Did you see them as synonymous before reading this chapter?
4. Have you seen someone forgive the way "Eve" did? Does this type of forgiveness seem out of reach? What does God say? (See Luke 6:37.)
5. The Greek word translated "forgiveness" means "free fully, relieve, dismiss, let die, pardon, divorce, loose, and set at liberty." Which of these definitions best describes the way you forgive?
6. Do you need to join the Flushing Brigade? When will you do it? (See Ps. 22:19 NLT.)

Chapter 5

Held Hostage by Assaulting Memories

I n this list of defensive hesitations to forgive, there is one excuse that is the most commonly expressed forgiveness blocker. In fact, it may represent the ultimate battle of ever really forgiving the offender. Can you guess which one it is?

1. The offense was too great.
2. **The memories of the offense are so vivid.**
3. The offense was repeated.
4. You want to make the person pay for the offense.
5. You are too angry to even consider forgiving this person.
6. The offender didn't say, "I am sorry."

Did you guess number two? Here is a place where sincere Christians, who want to forgive and walk in freedom, end up stuck and held hostage. This major hesitation comes because you are struggling with vivid memories of the offense and this causes you to ask: *How can I forgive what I can't forget?* A person's struggle with the memory of the offense keeps one chained to yesterday.

If a memory were simply the recollection of an event or past experience, it would not keep an offended person victimized. But memories are accompanied by companion emotions: resurrected hurt, disappointment, fear, anger, and shame. If memory were simply the capacity to store images, minus the corresponding negative feelings, this chapter would not be necessary. Unfortunately, while computers are wired to retain information for future retrieval—minus the emotions—humans are not! We have wiring that connects both the brain and the heart. Later in this chapter, we are going to look at emotional trauma and its impact on the brain.

Can I Forgive What I Can't Forget?

Is it possible to erase troubling memories from the "hard drive" of our minds? Can a human ever forget loss, betrayal, abandonment, abuse, or rape? If a person cannot forget, can she ever be expected to truly forgive? If memories, flashbacks, and dreams remain active, must a Christian remain handcuffed to the tyranny of his or her memory? How does a person move past assaulting memories?

Let me share what happened to me. In 1990, I was at a conference where the speaker said to the audience, "All of you out there who know Jesus and want a closer walk with the Lord, you'd better not be holding on to something that's coming between you and the Savior." I sat there thinking, *Don't look at me. Don't even think about pointing your finger at me!* The speaker continued: "Let the Lord reveal to you whether or not you are holding a grudge against somebody. Is there someone from the past who has hurt you through betrayal, slander, abandonment, rejection, or abuse? Are you thinking about someone who demeaned or marginalized you publicly?"

As the speaker continued to fire off these questions, people began to pop into my head, one by one, each matching one of the remarks he made. I could say yes to all of his questions. It was as though the speaker were reading a "hit list" of various hurts that I was hiding in my heart. With every example of offense, I could recall what I experienced, and I could actually visualize each perpetrator.

Many of those familiar faces were people from my family. I have shared with you the context of the home in which I was raised. But let me relate it to you through some other people's eyes. One year at a Christmas party for professional counselors in south Florida, a group began to discuss who would be on their top-ten lists for the most dysfunctional family: my family of origin was one of them.

As you can imagine, hearing about such a statement resurrected shame and self-contempt in me, but being the need-to-smile-and-hide-your-pain Christian at the time, I tucked the painful remark deep into my heart. My friend, who was one of those counselors, relayed the information, shaking her head and saying, "Jackie, you have the most amazing family!" And I thought, *Thanks. Amazing dysfunction!* How could so many people be that messed up—from one family? You know how families have a black sheep. Our family made up a whole flock of black sheep!

After the speaker finished his "hit list" of potential hurts from past offenses, he invited members of the audience to come forward for counseling and prayer. When I went to the front of the auditorium, a couple of older women approached me. I confessed to the women that my greatest source of past offense and hurt was my abusive father. The women said, "You've been forgiven so much, and you need to forgive your father. If he never repents, if he never owns what he's done to his children, you let it go, girl, or you're going to be sick your whole life." Frantically I responded, "I don't want to be sick, I want to be free! I want to be Jesus' slave, not my dad's slave anymore!"

I remember them praying over me while I cried out, "O Lord, by faith, right now, by faith I give the gift of forgiveness to my father"—and indeed, I was praying that by faith. Well, about a week later I was at Kmart during a Blue Light Special, and all of a sudden the most horrible memory of my father just surged over me. It was as if a bucket of slime had been poured on my head and was dripping down my body. My immediate thought was, *Oh no, it didn't take! Whatever those women prayed at that conference, whatever I prayed, we didn't get through. It didn't work!* I was hysterical inside. I started to cry out, right in the middle of Kmart (of course, cry out in prayer...not out loud, but in my soul), "God, I know I forgave my dad. I know I released him into Your wise and just hands, counting on You alone to handle his sin. What happened? Why do I feel like this?" I left the store grieved and discouraged. *How can I forgive what I can't forget?*

The 490 Principle

Then, several days later, Jesus gave me the most awesome gift in His Word, a gift that has helped this former hostage through hundreds of painful memories. He taught me the 490 Principle, which finally showed me what to do with the retrieved images and painful emotions. Look at what I read: "Peter got up the nerve to ask, 'Master, how many times do I forgive a brother or sister who hurts me? Seven?' Jesus replied, 'Seven! Hardly. Try seventy times seven'" (Matt. 18:21–22 THE MESSAGE).

The first observation I made was that Peter used the words *brother or sister* when he was speaking about needing to forgive a past hurt. I believe Peter used these terms because nobody can hurt you worse than a brother or sister can. Nobody can hurt you worse than someone who knows you, who loves you, who's connected to you either by the blood of your mother or by the blood of Jesus. When those who are closest to you offend you, you're pretty stunned.

I can clearly remember as a young Christian finding out that I was a part of the new "forever family," the body of Jesus. That meant I had all these brothers and sisters to love and be loved by. I was so excited! I was from such a crummy family, my heart-cry was "Bring on a good one!" And then, lo and behold, some of those Christians started acting like my lost siblings. Suddenly I thought, *I'm not sure this is such a good deal here. I thought God's children would be different from my natural siblings.* I was so disappointed when my spiritual siblings acted as unloving as my natural brothers and sisters did.

When Peter suggested forgiving a brother or sister *seven* times, he actually thought he was being generous. Peter knew that within the context of Judaism, forgiving three instances of hurt (see Amos 1:3; 2:6) was considered plenty. When Peter doubled the standard, he was being very magnanimous. When Jesus replied with "seventy times seven," His standard of countless times for forgiving one's brother was absolutely unprecedented and astonishing.[1]

If you forgive someone like your husband only seven times, you could conceivably run out of forgiveness by the end of a weeklong honeymoon! Let's face it: the most wonderful groom in the world will still need to be forgiven regularly by his wife—and vice versa. Great marriages are sustained by the ability to forgive again and again. Being good forgivers allows spouses to embrace their mates with all their flaws, facing the reality that we live outside the Garden of Eden.

Peter's suggestion to forgive seven times is not enough to handle the world in which we live and breathe. Jesus' reply was so much more realistic: "Hardly. Try seventy times seven." Jesus knew one could "hardly" make it through a week with a forgiving quota of seven instances per person.

Seventy Times Seven

When I first read and memorized this verse, I actually looked at the 490 number as a *literal* quota for forgiving someone. You may think this sounds naive, or even nuts! But I wanted to take God's Word at face value! So, I began to visualize people with these blinking units above their heads, like numerical halos. I would see one person with the blinking number of 110, another person with a blinking number of 56, and another at 270. My logical conclusion, of course, was that when the numerical halo started blinking 490, I'd say, "You're out of here! Strike 490 and you are out of the game!" I would conclude, *I don't have to forgive this particular person anymore.*

One day I was speaking with a friend on the phone. "Boy, my dad has just about exhausted his quota for forgiveness," I said. "He's almost hit 490." My friend was a marvelous Christian counselor, and she asked, "Jackie, what are you talking about?" I replied, "You've read that Scripture where Peter and Jesus are discussing forgiving a brother or sister, and Jesus replies that you only have to forgive them 490 times." I went on to describe those blinking lights I envisioned, measuring people's forgiveness levels.

My friend started to laugh, but her wisdom as a professional helped her to stop. She said gently, "Jackie, that 490 is 490 times for the same offense. Sometimes things that God lets happen to us are so horrible that the intensity of the event will make repetitive memories inevitable, so a person will be forgiving the same offense again and again. Even though the offense is past, the depth of the trauma keeps returning in the form of assaulting memories."

That day on the phone, my precious friend taught me the 490 Principle. When I hung up the phone, I was actually excited about my dreadful memory in Kmart that week. I realized that this intruding, offensive memory was not proof of my lack of forgiveness, but instead it was evidence of the depth of the assault I had experienced from my own father. From that day forward, whenever I faced a sudden memory or even a horrible dream, I remembered the 490 Principle and thanked the Lord both that I had forgiven, and that I knew how to forgive and release the person again.

Whatever the trauma you experience, you don't get over it in a minute. That terrifying memory will be played out in dreams, flashbacks, and memories at the most inconvenient times. For a girl who was date-raped, for example, the next time a guy asks her out, the simple invitation can trigger the most agonizing memory, and she has to forgive again. Her preparation for a date will involve not only physical preparation but also emotional preparation.

Jesus Addressed the Neurobiology
of Healing Trauma

Over the years, I have seen the 490 Principle provide such healing and liberty for those held hostage through uninvited memories. Forgiving again and again only strengthens one's capacity to be a great forgiver, and consequently a great lover of people.

At a 2003 conference on abuse (physical, verbal, sexual, spousal), Dr. Catherine Moritz spoke on spiritual healing. As she explained why healing is sometimes difficult, she explained the trigger points in the brain that are connected with memories and the slices of memory that keep past trauma current. Then she said something that almost caused me to jump to my feet and start cheering for the 490 Principle.

Catherine described the brain as an astounding organ that is constantly working to keep a state of homeostasis or equilibrium. In order for a person's mind to heal, homeostasis is required. The right side of the brain is where trauma is stored, and if the right side of the brain gets overloaded with too much pain, heartache, and trauma, we lose our emotional equilibrium. The brain begins to work through the conscious and subconscious to restore homeostasis, and this restoration will result in flashbacks, dreams, and memories that need to be recognized, sorted, and healed.

I got choked up as I realized that the 490 Principle in God's Word brings healing for our hearts as well as our minds. Our minds are restored to homeostasis through memories, and our hearts are restored to their necessary equilibrium as we become skilled forgivers.

Welcome Memories and Flashbacks as Emotional Gifts

As long as your brain is working, memories are inevitable—the good and the bad. Instead of resenting the bad ones as intruders, welcome them as part of the continuing process of forgiveness. When a difficult memory presents itself, and you process it in the context of previously forgiving the same offense, you can peacefully rejoice in the forgiveness you had already freely given, *and the memories about the particular trauma begin to subside.* Naturally, after experiencing this kind of liberation, I began to wonder if there is a correlation between refusing to forgive and the inability to be restored to emotional equilibrium. Not only does unforgiveness keep the offense alive, it also keeps the right side of our brains overloaded with trauma and drama.

As we've seen, one of the greatest apostles understood the incredible need for forgiveness: "If you forgive anyone, I also forgive him. And what I have forgiven—if there was anything to forgive—I have forgiven in the sight of Christ for your sake" (2 Cor. 2:10). I particularly appreciate the part of this verse where Paul says, "If you forgive anyone, I also forgive him." Paul was joining the Corinthian Christians in forgiving anyone they needed to; it's as if Paul was saying, "Me, too!" When someone is willing to forgive an offense, we need to shout, "Me, too!" Too often Christians keep offense alive by harboring unforgiveness even when their brothers and sisters have offered forgiveness. I have seen a woman forgive her unfaithful husband, but the rest of the family was not willing to say, "Me, too." Therefore they kept the offense alive, and no one was freed or healed.

We don't need to allow our memories to be tools in the hands of the scheming enemy of our souls. Memories will be triggered as long as we are breathing. But we are not powerless over their intrusion! We are not without direction. The 490 Principle was given to the very apostle who would have to live the rest of his life dealing with the memory of denying three times the precious Lord he so loved. We, like Peter, have been given the 490 Principle. We can outwit the enemy of our souls by applying this principle when confronted with a memory, flashback, or hurtful dream.

Isn't It Ironic?

Consider something a bit ironic. Peter asked his spiritual brother Jesus (see Matt. 18:21–22) how many times he should forgive an offending brother. Jesus gave Peter the 490 Principle; then Peter sinned against his spiritual brother Jesus by denying Him three times. Peter, the one instructed in the 490 Principle of forgiving, became the offending brother.

When Jesus rose from the dead, His message of forgiveness was clear. He said to the women who encountered their risen Lord, "Go and tell my brothers to go to Galilee; there they will see me" (Matt. 28:10). One may ask if Jesus included Peter in this group of brothers. The angel at the empty tomb answered this question when he said to the women, "Go, tell his disciples and Peter" (Mark 16:7).

Jesus had freely forgiven a brother who sinned against Him. I don't doubt that Peter lived the rest of his days with this bittersweet memory of forgiveness framing his life, allowing him to forgive others freely—even when they crucified him upside down (as legend has it).

I received this e-mail from someone who had attended my seminar on forgiveness:

> *Lately, I have been flooded with spam on our e-mail. I have been going through each one (very time consuming) and asking the companies to unsubscribe me to their e-mails. It is really quite simple. You type in your e-mail address and hit "Unsubscribe" and in twenty-four to forty-eight hours, they will stop bothering you. (We'll see if that's really true!)*
>
> *It struck me that this kind of illustrates forgiveness. Often the memories of past offenses flood our e-mail boxes in our brains. But we just need to type in our favorite verses on forgiving our enemies, etc., then hit "Unsubscribe." Now I know the memories may keep coming back, but with time they will lessen.*

One of my favorite teachers from college wrote a book about forgiving in which she so wonderfully addressed this reality of triggered memories from unexpected stimuli—pictures, holidays, or simply a person with the same name. Her remark about these memories validates the 490 Principle:

> Sometimes when we think the book is closed and forgiveness is complete, a sudden reminder of that thing which happened overwhelms and confuses: we experience again the hurt and anger that we thought was permanently discarded. When that happens, we must go back, not to the one who hurt us to open old wounds, but to the one who has the instant prescription—that balm in Gilead that brought healing the first time we needed it.[2]

Overreacting to a very simple incident, as I explained earlier, can often be traced to some buried hurt. This buried pain fuels disproportionate emotions and can certainly be the reason behind sensitivity to marginal offenses. These emotions can be resurrected through memories.

Instead of resenting memories, one can rejoice that God wants to free us from ruling emotions that are not healthy or beneficial to ourselves or those around us. So often when I teach on forgiveness, people remark to me afterward that they were having flashbacks while I was teaching. I now alert my audiences about the potential for this and tell them not to fear the memories. Rather, they should fear shoving down more pain that will eventually rise up to rule as a despot.

When a memory or flashback intrudes on your day, examine it and consider this: *Have I already forgiven this person and released this event? Or have I buried the hurt and anger, and am I still being ruled by what is buried?* As David Seamands wrote: "The submerged emotions rise up and express themselves in feelings of deep depression, rage, uncontrollable lust, inferiority, fear, loneliness, and rejection."[3]

Don't Let Memories Drag You Back into Rage

Returning memories and fresh details of offense can drag you back into the anger that once ruled you. This is all part of the process of forgiving. *Forgiveness is both instantaneous and continuous.* I forgive my offender instantaneously and then a few weeks or years later, through a vivid memory of the offense, I forgive again — and again (continuously).

A survivor of the Rwandan holocaust expresses this:

> My soul was at war with itself. I'd struggled so hard to forgive but now felt duped for having done so.... When

my neighbors whispered the stories of my family's sadistic murders in my ear, the feeling of hatred that I thought I'd banished from my soul sprang violently from the depths of my being with renewed vigor....I tossed and turned for hours....I rolled out of bed and got down on my knees. "Forgive my evil thoughts, God." A sudden rush of air flooded my lungs. I heaved a heavy sigh of relief. The anger that had gripped me like a returning malignancy was gone.[4]

This woman's courage to forgive what many would consider an offense too great, with memories far too relentless and vivid, is absolutely stunning.

The next time your brain sends you a memory, flashback, or dream, remember your need for homeostasis and rejoice that you know the 490 Principle. Practicing this principle is helping you achieve a PhD in Forgiveness—ultimate Christlikeness. And becoming experts in forgiveness frees us to be experts in loving others. Memories are not the enemy but a vehicle for truth in the innermost part of our souls.

MAKE IT PERSONAL

1. Discuss how memories keep one a victim of past offenses.
2. Has a recent memory flooded you with fresh hurt? What triggered it?
3. Is this the first time you considered Jesus' message in the context of forgiving the same offense, again and again? How liberating to you is the prospect of the 490 Principle? (See Matt. 18:21–22.)
4. Is it liberating to you that memories are part of the *healing*

process? Why or why not? If liberating, explain in your own words how freeing it is.

5. "Sometimes things that God lets happen to us are so horrible that the intensity of the event will make repetitive memories inevitable, so a person will be forgiving the same offense again and again." Can you see this idea's application in your own experience?

6. Can you share an intense memory and how you might apply the 490 Principle in relation to it?

7. What did you think about the neurobiology of the healing of your brain through memories and forgiveness?

8. Are you ready to welcome memories as emotional gifts? Why or why not? (See 2 Cor. 2:10, 11.)

Chapter 6

Held Hostage by Repeated Offense

E xcuses for unforgiveness:

1. The offense was too great.
2. The memories of the offense are so vivid.
3. **The offense was repeated.**
4. You want to make the person pay for the offense.
5. You are too angry to even consider forgiving this person.
6. The offender didn't say, "I am sorry."

People often hesitate to forgive because they are aggravated—
you might even say they are *exasperated*—with repeated
offense. Imagine it like this: people who focus on what someone did to them are like people who carry around an "offense
calculator." They continually keep tabs, and they can tell you
the last time he said this or did that—as well as what he was

wearing at the time! They're constantly keeping ledgers, whole books of them. I call these "grudge books."

Entries in Grudge Books

Grudge books can take different forms. For the accountant in us, they're the ledgers in which we keep meticulous accounts of offenses. For the creative writer in us, they take on the dramatic flair of a novel or a play. Sometimes we're feeling crafty and create elaborate scrapbooks or photo albums filled with the memories of our grudges, and sometimes our grudge books are just our personal journals: "Dear Diary, can you *believe* she snubbed me *again*?!" Look around your house. Do you have any grudge books lying around?

Actually, we *all* have these books—all human beings are inclined to remember offenses. I know people who keep records of things that have been done to them in embossed, laminated albums! Their holiday scrapbooks aren't filled with happy photos of the family, they're filled with images of all the ways things did *not* go as planned or people did *not* act the way someone hoped they would. But we need to be reminded that keeping grudge books is in direct disobedience to what God says. First Corinthians 13:5 tells us that "love keeps *no record* of wrongs" (emphasis added). (Gulp!) That is easier said than done.

I looked up the verb *record* and it means "a mind occupied with calculating."[1] When we keep records, our minds are given over to rehearsing the details of the offensive incident. We are preoccupied with calculating what's been done to us. What does your mind do with repeated calculation? It moves it to a place of effective memorization.

Who Suffers?

The saddest aspect of being a public accountant of people's offenses is that there's only one person who experiences the occupational fallout—you! The offender is not distracted by thoughts of the offending incident. What I learned was that *the record I was keeping was not hurting any of the other people involved; it was hurting only me.* It was making *me* sick. You cannot change someone for the better by holding a grudge. Grudges change only you—for the worse.

We need to be aware that if we are fastidious record keepers, we are probably better grudge bearers than forgivers. The grudge book gets heavier with every passing day as we record daily grievances from living in a damaged world. I want to encourage you to frame it this way: when a person commits another offense, it simply means this person still has a pulse. Another offense offers us another opportunity to forgive.

Warning: it is critical to differentiate between forgiving repeated offenses and enduring an abusive situation. A woman should never continue to live with a man who is abusing her or her children because she knows how to forgive him again. This woman will need to forgive him—*after* she calls the police and has him escorted from their home. Moreover, she will have to forgive him as she fills out a request for a restraining order against him and then another 490 times!

In Genesis we read of how Joseph's brothers sold him into slavery because they were jealous over their father's attention. Years later, when the family was reconciled, Joseph was good to his brothers and forgave them. But when Isaac died, the brothers began to worry: "When Joseph's brothers saw that their father was dead, they said, 'What if Joseph holds a *grudge*

against us and pays us back for all the wrongs we did to him?'"
(Gen. 50:15, emphasis added).

It was no stretch for his brothers to think Joseph had been
harboring a major grudge against them. How ironic it is that,
instead of payback, Joseph comforted and cared for his brothers!
He showed ultimate Christlikeness—he was a great forgiver!
Joseph reassured them and "spoke kindly to them" (Gen. 50:21).
His compassion displayed his forgiveness. Before his brothers
came to Egypt, Joseph had already released the offense.

How do I know Joseph did not keep an extensive grudge
book with his brothers as the main characters? The answer to
this is revealed in the names of Joseph's two sons, Manasseh
and Ephraim. The names he chose for his sons show not only
that Joseph released and forgot (forgave) past hurts but also
that Joseph saw his suffering as something fruitful in God's
hands:

> Before the years of famine came, two sons were born to
> Joseph by Asenath daughter of Potiphera, the priest of
> On. Joseph named his firstborn Manasseh and said, "It
> is because God has made me forget all my trouble and
> all my father's household." The second son he named
> Ephraim and said, "It is because God has made me fruit-
> ful in the land of my suffering." (Gen. 41:50–52)

Joseph's children were a display of his victory over the
offenses of his past. Unfortunately, when we don't forgive, our
children can be a display of the bitterness and hurt of our pasts.
How do our children assimilate our bitterness and unforgiveness? They discover it in our grudge books.

Generational Inheritance

Do you know who reads your grudge book? Your mate and children and friends—they all know who has hurt you and whom you are holding a grudge against. When I was a little girl, my mother would tell me stories about how her mother-in-law (my grandmother) hurt her. I never liked this particular grandmother because of those terrible stories. I took up my mother's offense by effectively memorizing the text of the grudge book she had penned on her soul and copied to mine.

My own children never knew the details of the deep hurt that my mother-in-law caused me. From time to time, they may have caught a brief glimpse of the journaling in my grudge book, but they never had free access to read and reread the pages of that book because I learned to forgive my mother-in-law. The mental journaling in a grudge book ceased!

In the third book of the Bible, we are warned: "Do not seek revenge or bear a grudge against one of your people, but love your neighbor as yourself. I am the LORD" (Lev. 19:18). To *bear* a grudge is to take care of it as though it were valuable. In Hebrew the word translated "bear" means to "guard, reserve and cherish."[2] How scary to think that one's grudges can be cherished like fond memories of yesterday.

When we read the whole of Leviticus 19:18, we grasp the reality that the one toward whom we cherish a grudge is not one we are loving as we love ourselves. When we hold on to cherished grudges, they can actually become family heirlooms that are passed down to future generations. I have a dear friend whose siblings refused to forgive their father, and the anger they harbored for him now possesses the hearts of the grandchildren. Not only do they possess the anger, it possesses them. Ironically, however, the grandchildren don't hate their grandfather, the object of their parents' hate—they hate their parents. The sons hated their father and never forgave him, and now *their* sons hate *their* fathers!

Here is a fact: we can't carry hate in our souls for someone without the toxic waste from this grudge harming our children and consequently angering them toward us. Consider the amount of prejudice that passes from generation to generation. Could it be that such anger is kept alive through the cherishing of grudges toward a certain group of people?

A story in the book of Judges reveals the impact of a three-hundred-year-old grudge. The Ammonites attacked Israel because Israel had taken land from them three hundred years prior. Jephthah, a mighty warrior, confronted the king of the Ammonites for attacking because of a centuries-old incident: "For three hundred years Israel occupied Heshbon, Aroer, the surrounding settlements and all the towns along the Arnon. Why didn't you retake them during that time? I have not wronged you, but you are doing me wrong by waging war against me. Let the LORD, the Judge, decide the dispute this day between the Israelites and the Ammonites" (11:26–27).

A grudge held in the heart of the Ammonites passed through three hundred years of family inheritance and fueled an attack on Israel. This is just one example of passing a grudge from one generation to another. Consider the complexity of the generational grudges that keep the conflict alive in the Middle East to this day!

What Nourishes a Grudge

What is it that keeps grudges alive? Besides unforgiveness, pride also nurses a grudge. To use some other metaphors, pride cherishes the grudge books of your soul and dusts them regularly. Pride is the interior coach encouraging you to develop a grudge you feel toward an offender. Pride is a trained CPA, keeping account of all the offenses you will rehearse in the presence of anyone who will listen.

My husband and son went to Africa for a mission project in 1994. While they were there, they visited a very influential woman in Kenya and enjoyed a long conversation with her. Our fifteen-year-old son told her, "The Kenyans I have met have all been so extremely friendly to us." This gracious woman's response I have never forgotten: "When England gave Kenya its freedom, we decided as a country to release the anger and forgive the past and to move forward into a future of freedom." Freedom was determined not by England but by the Kenyans' choice to forgive a painful past. Rather than being arrogant by holding a grudge, these people decided to forgive and to become a nation characterized by forgiveness. They did this so that the voices of the past did not drown out God's voice in the present. God never consults our pasts to determine our futures, and neither should we (see Heb. 12:2).

Tell Your Story...but Be Careful

In all of this discussion about our grudge books, I need to make clear that it is utterly necessary for an offended person to *share* his or her grief. We should never hide in the frozen stoicism or buried denial we reviewed in earlier chapters. We need to speak about our pain not only with God but also with another person so that the healing may begin. This is actually a biblical process (see Gal. 6:2; James 5:13–16). This person should be a trustworthy pastor, counselor, or friend. If you have soul-shaking pain, however, make sure you see a professional Christian counselor who can walk you through the healing process.

Caution: if your grievance story becomes the *only* story you have to share with others, it becomes so deeply etched in your person that you see everything in life through the lens of the offense. It is like having a bent antenna and picking up static rather than clear sound on a consistent basis.

In addition to telling our grievance stories for the purposes of healing, there is a place for repeating them in order to encourage others to forgive freely. But honestly, a lot of that static we hear over the airwaves is just the repetition of grievance stories as a defense for unforgiveness. It is so like the flesh to play the offense over and over until it becomes so deeply imbedded that freedom to forgive is virtually unfathomable. We actually think that by etching the offense into our souls, we will be released from pain. Be careful. A grudge can become enormously hard to dislodge.

Have you ever met a divorcée who had such fresh rage toward the ex-spouse you assumed the divorce must have been recent, only to discover that it took place a decade ago? Allowing an event from a decade ago to cast a cloud over the present makes it rain on the day that God has blessed you with today. A grievance story without the frame of ultimate forgiveness only enrages those who are already struggling with being victims.

Therefore, when unforgiveness is exposed, our intent needs to be extraction, *not* the cultivation of a new level of rage toward the offender.

A dear friend reflected on her struggle to forgive:

One of the main reasons it is hard for me to forgive, especially someone who is a repeat offender, is because I think that by forgiving them I'm telling them what they did was not a big deal and that it's okay. I think that by holding on to my hurt, my anger, and my pride, I am making sure that...the person who hurt me realizes and remembers what they did and how bad it was. In my relationship with my brother, an area where I've needed to learn a lot of forgiveness, I thought that if I forgave him I would enable him to hurt me over and over because I was just going to forgive whatever he did.

I think forgiveness is also hard because it puts us in a constant state of vulnerability. I know that when I have to consciously pray through forgiving someone or telling someone that I forgive them, I am making myself vulnerable and acknowledging the hurt. Sometimes, without forgiveness you can pretend that you weren't really hurt at all.

I also think that I lack a proper view of forgiveness. I often don't forgive because I don't think the person "deserves" forgiveness. If I truly thought about and comprehended what God has forgiven me for, I think I would be more apt to forgive others. My improper view of the depth of my own sin deceives me into thinking that others do not "deserve" my forgiveness....

I have realized that I do not fully understand the depth and meaning of forgiveness and why we are supposed to forgive. I have often heard and been told that we do not always forgive for the sake of the other person, but we forgive so that we do not harbor feelings of hate or anger in ourselves. While I understand this, I often thrive on the feelings that come with "withholding" my forgiveness. It makes me feel like I have the power and control in the relationship with the other person and it's up to me whether or not we move forward.

—Courtney (2007 Wake Forest graduate)

Impact vs. Intent

Remember, people hurt you because, like you, they are far from perfect. They are wounded themselves. Forgive their incompleteness, their humanness. Leviticus 4:13–27 contains a provision for *intentional* and *unintentional* sins. We tend to assume that every offense is intentional. My dear friend Bobbe teaches people how to discern the difference between *impact* and *intent*. She encourages people to ask two questions in relation to each offense committed by a spouse, family member, friend, or coworker:

Impact: Do I feel hurt or offended?
Intent: Did he or she intend to hurt me?

When you've considered these two aspects of an offense, you can calmly respond to the offender, "I know you didn't *intend* to hurt me, but that remark really hurt my feelings!" Years ago I heard Joyce Meyer say, "Ninety-five percent of the things that people do to offend us were not even intended." So many offended people believe that the offender held meetings to plan how to humiliate them in front of coworkers. Or someone's husband lay awake all night planning to disappoint his wife by forgetting their anniversary—again. Yet we can choose to frame our response to impact and intent through the message of 1 Corinthians 13:7, which tells us that love "always protects, always trusts, always hopes, always perseveres."

Every offense or memory of offense offers us an opportunity to enhance our identity as people who forgive. Those who forgive embrace the chance for instruction in a current offense or the memory of a past offense.

Unforgiveness as Emotional Deformity

My dear friend Ruth wrote a great word picture for trying to live with a deep, unforgiven grievance: "It is like someone trying to clothe herself with a beautiful garment of compassion, kindness, and patience [who] has to yank and stretch it over this big, ugly lump on her back—a tumorous growth of forgiveness on hold."[3]

I think of the hunchback of Notre Dame, who hid from the view of others because of the shame of his deformity. I have to agree with Ruth: people harboring unforgiveness walk around with a deformity. Yet because of their attachment to this lump, when they are invited to have it removed so they can be healed, they insist on keeping it.

We can see this in the book of Ezra. The Levitical priests had been taken into captivity in Babylonia, and when the king finally granted them permission to leave, they opted to stay with what had become familiar: "I assembled the exiles at the Ahava Canal, and we camped there for three days while I went over the lists of the people and the priests who had arrived. I found that *not one Levite* had volunteered to come along" (Ezra 8:15 NLT, emphasis added).

Too often one's grievance story becomes one's only identity. The familiar prison of captivity seems safer than the leap of faith into the unknown that is required to forgive the offender. Early in my relationship with my husband, his mother's rejection of me became my own grievance story. This story resulted in years of a default setting on offense. The slightest hurt became a cancer of offense because of the unforgiveness that was feeding the tumor on my back. Not until I learned the principles in this book was I willing to submit to the complex surgery required to remove the huge tumor strangling my heart and mind. Unforgiveness never lies dormant—it always metastasizes into something more deadly.

When someone starts doing drugs at a young age, maturation is stunted. This is called *arrested development*. Some of my siblings started doing drugs as teens, and now as adults, they make decisions that are shocking for adults but typical of teenagers. When we choose not to forgive our offenders, this choice stunts our maturity emotionally and spiritually. Trauma in a person's life combined with the inability to work through the forgiveness process impedes the spiritual growth of the soul. I don't believe the Lord intends for us to be stuck.

Look at what the psalmist wrote: "A righteous man may have many troubles, but the LORD delivers him from them all" (Ps. 34:19). It has been said that we are the sum total of all that we have read. I believe we are also the sum total of all the books we have written—emotionally and mentally. We need to examine the content of these grudge books, since, as we know, they can be quite extensive.

So many people are stuck in unforgiveness their development is arrested, and the reason for this impasse can often be found in a popular book we'll call *The Diary of Why*, which includes questions such as *Why would he do such a thing? Why would she speak so harshly to me? Why was I overlooked when I was the obvious one for the task? Why does this person continue to offend and offend and never is stopped? Why does this relative have the freedom to ruin every holiday gathering? Why do Christians offend as freely as nonbelievers?* These are the kinds of questions millions ask as they struggle with the "why" behind an offense.

What happens when we get stuck writing and rereading this *Diary of Why?* When we continually rehearse the offense in search of why something happened, we are closed to forgiving the offender. This preoccupation with *The Diary of Why* leads to a pretty scary reality I've mentioned before—the reality that we are controlled by someone else. It is like having a pretty dog chain around our necks, but the name on the collar is not ours, it's the offender's. When I don't forgive someone, I am being walked around with a fancy dog collar with the offender's name on it, and I am being jerked around on the offender's leash.

The Suffocating Aspect of Unforgiveness

Even when you try to go in the right direction (emotional health), the offender can show up and the chain around your neck gets yanked! I was offended at one point by a particular Christian woman, and whenever her name was mentioned, that chain was yanked so hard it cut off my oxygen supply. With my oxygen supply compromised, you can only imagine the dizzying remarks I would make about her.

Are you being pulled about by a dog chain with an offender's name on it? Has someone just come to mind whose name you are never thrilled to hear? Believe me, I know what it's like when the name of that person not only chokes up on the collar around your neck but also robs you of the joy of the Lord. A dear friend of mine tells me that whenever she suggests that her granddaughter consider forgiving her father, the granddaughter actually gasps for breath as though she were choking. What does God say? "[God] will break the yoke of their slavery [the dog chains!] and lift the heavy burden from their shoulders" (Isa. 9:4 NLT).

The Hebrew word translated "offend" actually means "to bind tightly, writhing in pain, suffocating the victim."[4] Being offended can be suffocating, *yet remaining in bondage to the offender through unforgiveness is actually a strangling of oneself.* I have spent the last forty years (as a Christian) watching the slow suffocation of some of my siblings. As I learned how to forgive, I was able to remove the "noose" around my neck, and I have spent the last four decades praying and sharing and encouraging counseling so that my siblings could remove the suffocating noose around their necks by learning to forgive the unforgivable.

Two of my siblings are no longer alive. These could be their epitaphs:

> Blue-eyed blonde, smart, sensitive, artistic, unfairly compared to older sister, verbally and sexually abused by her dad. She got pregnant, dropped out of school, gave the baby up for adoption, began a love affair with alcohol...and committed suicide at the age of thirty-six.

> A son, tender, sensitive, kind, attentive, was verbally, physically, and sexually abused by his overbearing father. He got his sixteen-year-old girlfriend pregnant, dropped out of school, married her, suffered years of struggle with his self-image...and committed suicide at age forty.

The suffocation finally overwhelmed them, and both of them chose suicide over another day of being choked by their heart wounds. Living with unforgiveness is a slow suicide—a strangulation of hope.

One of the most painful experiences of my life is to see the unforgiving noose around the necks of those I love, and I long for them to be set free—no longer hostages to yesterday through unforgiveness.

These precious lives were suffocated through continual

entries in their *Diaries of Why*. Unquestionably they suffered mortal offenses. Nevertheless, whether grievances are marginal or mortal, when they are rehearsed as new journal entries that expand a copy of *The Diary of Why* from a pamphlet into a novel, they keep us captive to unforgiveness.

Are you being suffocated by a relentless *Why* in your heart? At some point, you need to take this particular book off the shelf of your heart, examine it, and determine to end the suffocation.

Unforgiveness Not Only Suffocates, It Also Isolates

I was having a discussion with two young women about the difficulty of forgiving a loved one who has offended us. The older girl, Faith, was trying to encourage the younger, Chelsea, to forgive her mom and start speaking to her again. I shared with this young girl how critical forgiveness is and how I, too, was concerned that she was being suffocated spiritually through the unforgiving attitude toward her mom.

Then Faith said to the struggling teen: "Ya know, unforgiveness is okay with itself. It abides alone—no room for love—no urgency to love." What an insight! The gap between the offender and the unforgiving one grows over time, and the isolation becomes a very dark canyon between loved ones.

Years ago I heard Ken Medema say at a concert, "People run back to yesterday and build higher walls of hate than there were before." Such walls can be constructed by piling up stacks of grudge books, including our *Diaries of Why*, about all the people in our lives who have offended us. The glue that holds the stacks together is our grievance stories, rehearsed daily. Forgiveness is the only way to stay out of the dragon's jaws (see

2 Cor. 2:10–11) and the only power to demolish this isolating wall. Job's life was hit by a tsunami of heartache, then a tornado of slanderous attacks from friends, and then Job burst out in complaint. "If my misery could be weighed and my troubles be put on the scales, they would outweigh all the sands of the sea. That is why I spoke impulsively.... Don't I have a right to complain?" (Job 6:2, 3, 5 NLT).

At the end of the book, God stated how angry He was with Job's friends, but not with venting Job. There is a time to vent and then a time to let go... forgive... move past... no longer be preoccupied with the offensive behavior of the offender.

We see *The Diary of Why* addressed in the book of Job. When you read the whole book, you have read dozens of *whys* that are never answered. Job was given a revelation rather than an explanation. At the end of the book, Job reflected, "Surely I spoke of things I did not understand, things too wonderful for me to know" (Job 42:3). Forgiveness is a "revelation" that exceeds explanation. Such insight is always a supernatural experience.

Forgiving the Unrepentant

In 2001 I taught a seminar on recovery from the impact of sexual abuse. I cautioned victims about confronting an unrepentant offender. I was making the point that we can forgive people who have not repented. Our forgiveness ends the suffocating control of the offenders. We are turning the debt of the offender over to God as the only One who can handle the injury involved.

After the conference, a woman sent an e-mail to me in which she mentioned the grief she experienced when she was urged to confront her offender. Her painful words ring in my ears even today. She said: "It took only one phone call to him—to wipe away all the years of therapy, reading the Bible, willingness to forgive—and turn me back into a raging, hurt, and angry victim—again. Talk about being reoffended."[5]

We will deal more with the concept of confronting the offender in a later chapter, but the point here is this: even if the offender doesn't recognize the trouble/pain he or she has caused (as they just stare with a blank expression while tears pour down your face), you can still extend forgiveness through Christ and refuse to hold on to the offense against you. In this circumstance you will be forgiving twice. You forgive the original offense and then forgive the denial of the offense.

Remember, forgiveness is always a *gift*...to the *offender* and to *yourself* as you release the offender into God's corrective care and then leave the suffocating noose behind.

Don't Let Anyone Use Up Your Three Inches

Do you ever wonder why God doesn't remove all the offensive people off the earth so that people can live in peace? One of the answers is that we would all be escorted off the planet, because we all offend at some time. There are people who seem to have advanced training in being offensive. The Word even warns us to "watch out" for those who tend to cause division through their offensiveness (Rom. 16:17). But forgiveness is never optional for the Christian.

Here is a verse I came upon that rocked my life perspective: "You have made my life no longer than the *width of my hand*. My entire lifetime is just a moment to you; at best, each of us is but a breath" (Ps. 39:5 NLT, emphasis added). After reading that verse, I got a piece of paper and traced my hand. Then I took a ruler and measured the width of my hand. It measured three and three-quarter inches. Wow, in comparison to the length of eternity, my three and three-quarter inches seemed microscopic. If most of us have only between three and six inches of life, what are we doing with this brief span of time on Planet Earth? Don't let your offender, the theme of your grudge books, use up the brief amount of time you have on this earth. When I let a grudge control my present, I am splitting a microscopic moment with the control of the offender.

To refuse to forgive is to continue to hurt oneself. Unforgiveness is a form of self-abuse. Victimized once, you can allow a lack of forgiveness to keep you stuck as a victim, holding on to a victim's identity. Instead, I finally learned how to release my victim mentality and claim the identity of one who forgives. I could abdicate the role of victim only by taking on the identity of the One who has forgiven me, and, consequently, I could forgive others freely. When I was living in a state of unforgiveness, it was a form of identity theft. I was not living like one who was forgiven. Victimization is identity theft of the believer who is to be identified by forgiveness, not suffocating self-pity.

Jan Silvious's book, *Look At It This Way*, opens with this chapter title: "This Is One Event in a Lifetime of Events." Jan offers this true observation:

> How you look at what happens to you will determine your success, your peace, and your sense of well-being and will ultimately tell the tale of a life *well lived or a life badly wasted*. . . . Anytime you allow *one* event or season of life to define you, your life, for all intents and purposes, *is over. It stops at that event*.[6]

God wants you and me to resist making a career of our victimization!

Do Not Join the VES (Victim Entitlement Society)

In the movie *Seems Like Old Times*, Charles Grodin makes a classic statement to Goldie Hawn: "If you can't learn to give up the past, you'll have to give up the present."

People who live in a perpetual state of victimization never receive all that comes with each new day, because they are dwelling in the past. They can't receive the grace that is available or God's faithfulness that is new each morning. They are so distracted by the past that the gift of the present eludes them.

If we choose to resist forgiving and remain victims, we will eventually find ourselves members of the VES (Victim Entitlement Society). The president of the VES is pride, in yet another of its roles. Pride maintains an overinflated view of what one deserves. This view leaves no room for any injustice or mistreatment—perceived or real. And it certainly holds a "no tolerance" policy toward repeated offense. In every speech by President Pride, the members of the VES are reminded of what they are entitled to: a fair, pain-free life!

The theme song for the VES is whining. Remember the perpetual chorus of this tune by the Israelites in the desert? Victims love to whine about how unfair life is to them. The demanding spirit in a victim helps a person sing this song with gusto. Such self-pity might appear as weak suffering, but truly, it is just inverted pride.

John Piper wrote:

> Boasting is the response of pride to success. Self-pity is
> the response of pride to suffering.... The reason self-pity
> does not look like pride is that it appears to be so needy.
> But the need arises from a wounded ego. It doesn't come
> from a sense of unworthiness, but from a sense of unrec-
> ognized worthiness. It is the response of unapplauded
> pride.[7]

In the process of South Africans' trying to heal from the
atrocities of apartheid, they created the Truth and Reconciliation Commission. Following are the suggested qualifications
for those who would participate:

> The commission should be comprised of victims, peo-
> ple whose lives had been ripped open by the horrors of
> oppression. But not arrogant victims, [Desmond Tutu]
> stated, not people looking for vengeance. Instead, Tutu
> said softly, these should be people who have the author-
> ity of awful experiences, experiences that educate them
> toward empathy, and yet still have within themselves
> hearts willing to forgive. This, he went on to clarify, could
> be accomplished only through a deeply buttressed spiri-
> tual life. These people will be wounded healers.[8]

This quote reminded me of the danger of the arrogance that
can fuel a lifestyle of victimization. Deeply offended persons
must resist joining the VES and pursue the healing and forgiveness that make them "wounded healers" rather than bitter,
cynical, arrogant victims.

A Bold Letter to an Adult Victim

I once knew a young woman who was stuck in a condo on 107 Victim Street. I had listened to her heartache for years, and one night after a lengthy e-mail, this is how I responded. I decided to keep it in a file so that I could share it with other victims who don't think they will ever have any identity other than that of *victim*.

> *Dear _____*
>
> *When I was thinking about your e-mail, a thought came to my mind: it is time to move from 107 Victim Street. It is now time to live like an adult in Jesus. The Lord gave me this acrostic:*
>
> *A = Act*
> *D = Directly*
> *U = Under*
> *L = Loving*
> *T = Training*
>
> *Jesus has been pouring into your heart His loving training, and He wants you to act under that guidance rather than react to every insensitive remark your offender or someone else makes.*
>
> *You are now capable of being an adult in Jesus, but sometimes you slip back into wanting the approval of humans rather than Him. We all do that! But every painful remark is a reminder of your need to practice this:*
>
> *Act*
> *Directly*
> *Under*
> *Loving*
> *Training*

> *Stop gauging your life on the approval or comments of mere men! All victims have a propensity toward self-pity, and as Oswald Chambers wrote, "Give sympathy to self-pity and you escort them to their death-bed."*[9]

In his wonderful book *Ruthless Trust*, Brennan Manning describes self-pity as the archenemy of trust and encourages the believer to set a time limit on self-pity. Why set a time limit on self-pity? Because it doesn't remain stagnant, it grows into a "deadly malignancy."[10]

From Victim to Victor

One summer I studied the life of the writer Hannah White-hall Smith, who could easily have used several painful events in her life to remain a victim. Her parents rejected her, her husband was unfaithful, and three of her children couldn't tolerate her passionate love for God. This victim of very hurtful situations chose to forgive her offenders and walk in God's love. This woman went from victim to victory because of her deep faith. Ironically, amid heartbreak, Hannah wrote the classic *The Christian Secret of a Happy Life*. God profoundly used her life because she didn't let others' cruel choices determine how she would live.

If you are wrestling with letting go of your victimization, of the pain of repeated hurts, remember: to *struggle* to do what is right is not extraordinary. Jesus, the perfect Lamb of God, wrestled in the Garden of Gethsemane (see Matt. 26) in response to the painful script in front of Him. The wrestling was not sin. Wrestling to do what is right is human, but wrestling ceases to be just human and moves into sin when we join the VES.

The only answer to our wrestling is to finally submit to God's will. To finally forgive is the only way to end the wrestling and the suffocating victimization. As I've said, continuing not to forgive is a form of self-abuse and self-victimization. If you have recognized the choking sensation of this dog chain, it has been revealed so you can remove the collar—by forgiveness.

"The surest display of the greatness of the glory of the grace of God...is the slaughter of the best being in the universe for millions of undeserving sinners."[11] Jesus, the best being in the universe, was slaughtered for the undeserving. When you consider not forgiving the "undeserving one" because he or she has repeated their hurtful ways toward you, remember Jesus, who was slaughtered for you and me—the undeserving ones!

What merciful irony that the victim is in the place of mediating between God and man, the very place that Jesus took on the cross. If you can grasp this privilege, forgiveness will become a pattern for living, for forgiving freely, and for loving. "Your salvation will come like the dawn, and your wounds will quickly heal. Your godliness will lead you forward, and the glory of the LORD will protect you from behind" (Isa. 58:8 NLT).

MAKE IT PERSONAL

1. Do you keep a mental photo album with pictures of people you are holding grudges against? Or have you been a CPA of a particular person's offenses against you? Who is in your album or ledger? How have you kept track of others' offenses? (See 1 Cor. 13:5.)

2. Previously had you considered that others are influenced by the content of one of your grudge books? Who in your life

knows about some of the grudges you are recording mentally and emotionally? What might be the result of others' sharing your resentment? (See Lev. 19:18.)

3. What role does pride play in a person's keeping a grudge book? (See James 4:6.)

4. Do you know someone whose only identity is that of being a victim? Do you know someone who defends his or her right to have extensive grudge book entries? Describe his or her personality. Do you enjoy being around him or her?

5. Define the difference between a grievance story that encourages others to forgive in contrast to the grievance story that glorifies victimization.

6. Have you found yourself stuck in the *Diary of Why* this year? Do you know someone else who is stuck? What can you do to get free? (See Job 42:3; Ps. 39:5–7.)

7. Did this chapter encourage you to start forgiving an offender so you can remove the suffocating dog chain from around your neck? How and when will you do this? (See 1 Cor. 13:7; Ps. 34:19.)

8. Have you been a member of the VES (Victim Entitlement Society)? Reread the letter to the adult victim. Do you think it is fair or too harsh? Does it speak to you? (See Isa. 58:8, 9.)

Chapter 7

Held Hostage by Revenge Fantasies

Excuses for unforgiveness:

1. The offense was too great.
2. The memories of the offense are so vivid.
3. The offense was repeated.
4. **You want to make the person pay for the offense.**
5. You are too angry to even consider forgiving this person.
6. The offender didn't say, "I am sorry."

In the previous chapter we addressed the problem with repeated offenses and how, instead of forgiving, we develop grudges that actually hold us captive to our offenders. The grudge books we write, the ledgers of wrongs we keep, are the material that helps fuel what this chapter will address: revenge.

Revenge is our desire for justice, our desire to make offenders pay for their relational crimes against us. When I long to expedite retaliation against my offender, I have moved from the role of offended to the role of God and judge. Even people who don't even know God's Word can quote, "Vengeance is mine; I will repay, saith the Lord" (Rom. 12:19 KJV); and "To me belongeth vengeance, and recompense" (Deut. 32:35 KJV).

Revenge is birthed in the heart, cultivated by the stories in our grudge books and put into action through various means of payback. This payback can be as simple as never returning a person's calls to severe slander that costs him or her a career. Another popular form of revenge many wives use is the infamous "Not tonight, honey; I have a headache." You know what I mean; you want them to suffer a little, sweat it... and then you'll forgive them. We have ways to make husbands pay for hurting and disappointing us. The next time a wife says she has a headache, the husband should ask, "What did I do to offend you?"

A friend wrote me about the emotions that create the desire for revenge:

> *Forgiveness does not come easily. In fact, it's probably one of the hardest things in life to do. When I'm hurt by someone, my sinful flesh takes over, manifesting itself through ugly thoughts of pride, retaliation, anger, and self-pity. I fight forgiving. After all, I was offended, violated, insulted, and it's painful. Pity comes first. Then anger joins the ranks.*
>
> *This army of ugliness marches in step faster than I can believe. It fortifies my hurt and the thoughts become more intense. Pride marches alongside the pity and anger. Oh, how I want to retaliate. My anger grows deeper. Revenge now marches in front. And the commander of the army, the devil himself, makes me think this is good. He makes me think that*

*if I forgive, I'm a real spiritual wimp, and that I must fight
back. If I listen to the enemy, he makes me think I'm so much
better than the offender.*[1]

Brothers and Boomerangs

In Leviticus we read, "Do not hate your brother in your
heart.... Do not seek revenge or bear a grudge" (19:17–18).

Consider the grudge and hatred brewing in Absalom's
heart after he found out that Amnon raped his sister Tamar.
Although he remained silent, the hatred grew and a plan of
revenge was birthed. "Absalom never said a word to Amnon,
either good or bad; he hated Amnon because he had disgraced
his sister Tamar" (2 Sam. 13:22). Eventually the hatred resulted
in murder.

Not all heart hatred results in murder, but murder is not the
only death. There are deaths of relationships—which can be
resurrected only by a miracle of God. "A brother offended is
harder to be won than a strong city: and their contentions are
like the bars of a castle" (Prov.18:19 KJV).

A woman I know went to a funeral where, in the first row,
the father and brothers were weeping for their deceased son
and brother. The woman was really touched by the tears that
the father and brothers were shedding so freely. She thought,
Look at that expression of love for this brother and son. Later at
the gathering she found out why they were weeping so much.
They were living with the consequences of creative revenge. This
father and sons had become angry at the one brother over a
business situation, and they had shut him out in silence. They
worked in the same building, lived in the same neighborhood,
and hadn't talked to this man for more than a year.

Revenge is a dangerous boomerang that eventually harms the one who perpetrates the vengeful behavior. Ultimately, these men were filled with regret and deep grief for holding such a grudge against a family member. They violated the warning in Leviticus, and they live today with the guilt of such foolish revenge. You can throw something hateful at the one who offended you, but it ends up swinging right back into your life. I would rather be chased by God's blessings than by a boomerang heading straight for my head. "Trouble chases sinners, while blessings reward the righteous," says Proverbs (13:21 NLT).

Remember the verse in Leviticus that warns of revenge and grudges toward relatives (19:18)? Absalom had disregarded this part of the Torah in order to plan the murder of his brother. I have the dearest friend who is a champion for God. Recently she said something that made us both laugh, but it reveals a typical form of revenge: "I will forgive her [a particular family member]; I just don't want to talk with her ever again." Sound familiar?

Exposing Creative Revenge

During one of the angriest moments of my life, when I wanted nothing more than to exact revenge, God taught me a very powerful lesson. I was mentoring a young mother who was a new believer. One day she called me, crying, saying that a woman we both knew had insulted me horribly to her mother. What made the insult so grievous to us was that this young mom and I had been praying together weekly for the salvation of her mother, and now her mother thought I was a fraud.

When she shared what this woman had said to her mother, I said, "I need to get off the phone because I'm going to drive to her office and knock her jaw straight through her brain!" Can you imagine the thoughts going through this young Christian's mind? She had just heard her mentor say, "I need to get off the phone because I'm going to go knock her out!" What a great testimony I was at that moment.

So, I was running through my house, trying to find my keys, when this thought was dropped in my heart: *Look at Romans 12.* I thought, *I'm not reading the Bible right now! I will repent and ask forgiveness later, but she has to pay now.* But as I continued to search for my keys, I kept hearing, *Look at Romans 12.* Well, there were no keys on the counter, but there was my Bible. So I opened it to Romans 12, and the first passage I saw was:

> Do not take revenge, my friends, but leave room for God's wrath, for it is written: "It is mine to avenge; I will repay," says the Lord. On the contrary: "If your enemy is hungry, feed him; if he is thirsty, give him something to drink. In doing this, you will heap burning coals on his head." Do not be overcome by evil, but overcome evil with good. (Rom. 12:19–21)

The phrase "leave room for God's wrath" stuck out like a big, blinking message. Suddenly I had this picture in my mind. I saw a room with a window cut out so you could see into it, and inside was the woman who had insulted me. My first thought was, *Let me in there! Get the door open, I'm going to knock her out!* Then it was as if the Lord whispered to my heart, *"Jackie, do you want to go in there—or would you like Me to take care of her?"* And I thought, *Go get her, King Jesus!* I could just see Him stepping into the door and boom! She would be annihilated.

Then I read the phrases, "If your enemy is hungry, feed him; if he is thirsty, give him something to drink....Overcome evil with good." I thought, *Oh, I don't know if I can go there, Lord. I won't kill her, but don't make me do something nice for her.* And I heard Him say, *"Go to Luria's and buy that frame you looked at last week. Have it gift-wrapped and then take it to her husband's office."* (I think the Lord suggested her husband's office as a safer way of delivering the gift.)

As I was driving to the store, I was talking to myself. *I'm giving her a gift? She insulted me!* Then I was reminded of the Scripture "Bless those who curse you" (Luke 6:28); *curse* means "to mistreat through speaking maliciously against you."[2] Well, this woman certainly spoke maliciously (she has never been a fan of my faith in Jesus).

"Bless those who curse you." Do you know that the word *bless* means "to call down divine favor"?[3] When someone hurts me, my first response is not to bless or to call down favor. I think about calling down holy fire.

I bought the gift and delivered it. As I was walking back into my house, my phone was ringing, and it was my young Christian friend, concerned about what I did to the woman. She very meekly asked, "Did you knock her out in the parking lot?" And I responded, "No, I'm the one who got knocked out." "Did she hit you?" "No, the Lord led me to read Romans 12." So I read her the passage, and she said "Well, what did you do in response?" I said, "I went and bought her a gift."

As you can imagine, my mentee was very surprised at my behavior. The Lord brought to mind later that we talk so much about the Scriptures, yet the power of the Scriptures is truly intensified when we live out their truth in front of people. Now, we know the Word of God doesn't *need* us, it's plenty powerful, but if we cooperate with it and obey it, you talk about the lid being taken off the joy! Jesus said in John 17, "[Father,] I have manifested Your name to the men whom You gave me out of the world" (NASB). *Manifest* means "to pull the lid off."[4] When you live the truth, you pull the lid off and the glory is released. Obey Him, beloved.

Later that week, my mentee shared with her mom my response to being insulted, and her mother was absolutely blown away. God went on to use my proper response as the strongest witness of God's Word in her life. Her doubts were replaced with newfound respect for her daughter's "God friend," which she called me from that moment on.

Forgiving Can Be Tough Work

Forgiving often reveals things about ourselves we may not want to look at. The idea that revenge is an easy way out is a lie. Even the greatest prophetic writer of the Old Testament struggled with the supposed waste of his good efforts: "My work seems so useless! I have spent my strength for nothing and to no purpose. Yet I leave it all in the LORD's hand; I will trust God for my reward" (Isa. 49:4 NLT). When you think that your hard work of forgiving is a waste and that revenge would be so much simpler, remember: your struggle is ultimately a struggle to trust God with resolution, justice, and rewards.

We need to throw off our tendencies to get even and make our enemies squirm and put on the new way of relating to relational crimes. "He will not crush the weakest reed or put out a flickering candle. He will bring justice to all who have been wronged" (Isa. 42:3 NLT).

Lay down your instrument of revenge and pick up your white flag of surrender to God, who will orchestrate the payback and bring the relief that your soul needs. "God is just: He will pay back trouble to those who trouble you and give relief to you who are troubled" (2 Thess. 1:6–7).

Revenge: An Ancient Hostility

Look at Ezekiel 25:12–13: "This is what the Sovereign LORD says: 'Because Edom took revenge on the house of Judah and became very guilty by doing so, therefore this is what the Sovereign LORD says: I will stretch out my hand against Edom.'" God stretches His hand out against those who take revenge. This is not a loving caress but a hand of discipline (see Heb. 12:6).

Revenge does not always have anything to do with a recent incident of offense. The conflict in the Middle East is a classic example of an ancient offense. Ezekiel continues:

> This is what the Sovereign LORD says: "Because the Philistines acted in vengeance and took revenge with malice in their hearts, and with ancient hostility sought to destroy Judah, therefore this is what the Sovereign LORD says: I am about to stretch out my hand against the Philistines." (25:15–16)

Again we read about God's outstretched hand of judgment, which is *not* the hand I want to encounter. I want the hand that lifts me from my hurt and despair to stand on the Rock of my salvation.

God was going to punish the Edomites and the Philistines for acting with revenge fueled by malice in their hearts. And while they may have charged into battle with spears and swords, revenge was their battle cry and malice was the strength pumping through their limbs. Understandably, such a literal battle may seem too far-fetched for you to even relate to, but most likely you have charged into emotional battles with malice fueling your strength and revenge setting your goal.

In Ephesians Paul mentioned that we often grieve the Holy Spirit with malice. Such ill will toward a person who has offended us results in our own illness. My desire to harm the offender actually harms my relationship with the Holy Spirit who dwells within me. That is a dangerous boomerang! Instead, Paul encouraged us, "Do not grieve the Holy Spirit of God, with whom you were sealed for the day of redemption. Get rid of all bitterness, rage and anger, brawling and slander, along with every form of malice" (Eph. 4:30–31).

Maybe you need to consider the residue of ill will (malice) that is still floating around in your heart. Ask the Lord right this moment to bring to light any free-floating malice that may still be in your soul toward someone who hurt you; and ask the Lord to help you be willing to get rid of it. Send it away—release it.

Nurse a Grudge and Cause a Beheading

In the book of Mark we read about Herod's wife, Herodias: "Herodias nursed a grudge against John and wanted to kill him. But she was not able to, because Herod feared John and protected him, knowing him to be a righteous and holy man" (6:19–20). Herodias was angry at John the Baptist because John had confronted Herod about the sin of taking his brother's wife in marriage. Her grudge erupted at her husband's birthday party:

> On his birthday Herod gave a banquet for his high officials and military commanders and the leading men of Galilee. When the daughter of Herodias came in and

> danced, she pleased Herod and his dinner guests. The
> king said to the girl, "Ask me for anything you want, and
> I'll give it to you."... She went out and said to her mother,
> "What shall I ask for?" "The head of John the Baptist," she
> answered. (Mark 6:21–24)

The consequence was John's beheading. What is so interesting is that Herodias's daughter was the instrument of her revenge. Remember in chapter 5 I stated that our children read our grudge books? Well, Herodias's daughter read the clear instruction in Herodias's grudge book: *John the Baptist deserves to die!*

Isn't it amazing that one woman's grudge had the power to convince a king to kill a man? Herodias finally got the perfect opportunity to exercise the revenge muscle of her nursed grudge.

Popular Forms of Revenge

I wonder whom my revenge will behead. How much harm has been caused by festering grudges? How many marriages have ended because of nursed grudges that climaxed in the revenge of divorce proceedings? What about the countless holidays ruined by revenge behavior among family members? I wonder how much religious slander—sanctified gossip—in the guise of prayer requests has sent a deathblow to a struggling Christian.

Let's consider that last one: the subtle manifestation of revenge through the vehicle of gossip or slander. I can't even number the times that I have gossiped, not because I was bored or too chatty, but because I was offended and I had not forgiven the offender. I found satisfaction in hurting the reputation of the offender through gossip (see Prov. 11:13; 20:19). Gossip is a common means of getting even and making people pay for the harm they have caused us, but it can actually lead to close friends becoming separated (see Prov. 16:28). When we find that gossip is a delicious morsel, satisfying our revenge taste buds, we must recall that the mouth speaks from what the heart is full of—heart-crushing bitterness (see Prov. 18:8; 26:22).

Note these words of wisdom:

> When we allow an offense to remain in our hearts, it causes serious spiritual consequences. In [Matthew 24:10, 12] Jesus named three dangerous results: betrayal, hatred and cold love. When we are offended with someone, even someone we care for, we must go to them. Otherwise, we begin to betray that relationship, talking maliciously behind their back to others, exposing their weaknesses and sins. We may mask our betrayal by saying we are just looking for advice or counsel, but when we look back, we see we have spoken negatively to far too many people. Our real goal was not to get spiritual help for ourselves but to seek revenge toward the one who offended us.[5]

Another popular form of revenge is sarcasm. "Scar-chasm" is what we call it in our house. It appears clever and witty but is, in fact, the lowest form of communication—and a reflection of an angry and offended heart!

One of the most tragic revenge scenarios I have ever heard of concerned the author Ernest Hemingway. His mother was so furious that he did not go to college she not only threw him out of the house, but on his twenty-first birthday, she sent him a package. In the package was the gun that his father had used to commit suicide. The mother wrote these words: *"I thought you'd want this."*

How could a mother be that hateful to her child? Anger and revenge are so blinding that they can change a person into an emotional monster. Hemingway later committed suicide, as did two of his siblings, Ursula and Leicester.[6]

You don't need to hire a professional hit man to hurt another human being for an offense. All humans have creative ways to expedite revenge. If you're looking to make a person squirm, one of the easiest ways is by not accepting their remorse or apology. I have met hundreds who refuse to accept a person's apology. These unforgiving people continue to nurse the hurt and grudge, which maintains the emotional gap between offender and offended. I know relatives who have not spoken in years. Such prolonged silence is creative revenge.

Revenge and the Flesh

We recently watched a movie depicting a key character on a mission of revenge. The title of the movie was *V for Vendetta* — hence the premise. A line spoken by the lead character caused me to run for pen and paper. The man who was designing his complex blueprint for revenge defended his right, saying, "What was done to me, created me." Isn't that a profound defense? A revenge-driven victim living life stimulated by his justifiable rage. I know Christians who have not only had revenge fantasies but have orchestrated some serious payback to other people, even in the area of slander. Revenge is ugly graffiti all over the grace of God.

In our flesh, we hesitate to lay down our weapon of revenge because of the injustice of it all. The situation seems unjust only because we are not trusting God to enact judgment against the offender. We may think that God is too busy to avenge our offenses or He isn't moving fast enough for our taste. We are terrified that the offender is going to be acquitted and that the case is going to be thrown out by the judge. So we take matters into our own hands.

I read a story about a mother and daughter uttering words of forgiveness in a courtroom:

> Sitting in her small blue wheelchair at the front of a Boston courtroom, Kai Leigh Harriott struggled to hold back her tears. Then she looked directly at the man whose bullet left her paralyzed nearly three years ago and spoke, loud and clear. "I forgive you, Anthony Warren," said Kai, 5. "What you done to me was wrong, but I still forgive you."
>
> Led from the courtroom in handcuffs the day Kai forgave him, Warren paused to apologize to the family. He and Tonya (mother) hugged. "I knew from the time Kai got shot that I had to forgive him," says Tonya. "For God to heal her, for her to stay alive, vengeance wasn't mine to take."[7]

I was deeply impacted by the mother's remark. This mother understood that she and her daughter, Kai, could live either in an eternal spirit of revenge or forgive and be free even while Kai was confined to a wheelchair. Kai's body is already confined by paralysis, but to not forgive would confine her soul to paralysis as well. Her mom's encouraging good example is a rebuke to many of us who still toy with revenge fantasies.

Forgiveness Is the Best Revenge

Take comfort that forgiveness is the better way. Two powerful passages from the book of Isaiah can be summarized with this simple promise: you can freely forgive, knowing that God will make it up to you (see 40:10; 61:7).

When I insist on revenge, I risk canceling the blessing that God has for me. Blessings chase the righteous, but blessings slam on their brakes in the presence of sprouting revenge!

I could write a novel-length book on the many ways God has made up for the pain in my life. One of my favorite recent stories has to do with an adoptive grandfather.

Best-selling author Chuck Snyder shared in one of his books about a special mailbox in the garden at his home. This mailbox has the names of all his grandchildren on it. Whenever Chuck knew his grandkids were coming over, before he went to work, he would make up individual gift envelopes for each of them. Each envelope would have a note from "BaPa," candy, and a few dollars. After I read this story, I wrote Chuck a letter about how deeply his love for his grandchildren touched my heart.

A couple of weeks later, I received a special gift envelope that had a note, candy, three dollars, and a Polaroid picture. Do you know what was in the photograph? The picture was of a garden with a mailbox and guess whose name was added to the mailbox? Mine! That loving gesture came to me not only from Chuck Snyder. That loving gesture came from God, who again is "making it up to me." As a child I was dreadfully shamed by a man; but as an adult, I continue to be healed by loving, honoring men—like BaPa.

God Has Not Forgotten What the Offender Did

Sometimes when we don't see people punished for what they did to us, we want to help God out with the punishment. I have learned when I am tempted to get revenge, I must consider my revenge fantasy and then choose to pray for *God's* remembrance of the offense. We see an example of this in Nehemiah: "Remember, O my God, all the evil things that Tobiah and Sanballat have done. And remember Noadiah the prophet and all the prophets like her who have tried to intimidate me" (6:14 NLT). I found it so interesting that Nehemiah prayed that God would remember the offenses of his enemies. As if God could ever forget what people do against His children! It is not unusual for the offended to ask God to remember retribution and justice. Even in the book of Revelation there is a reference to the martyred ones' asking God when revenge will be expedited:

> When he opened the fifth seal, I saw under the altar the souls of those who had been slain because of the word of God and the testimony they had maintained. They called out in a loud voice, "How long, Sovereign Lord, holy and true, until you judge the inhabitants of the earth and avenge our blood?" Then each of them was given a white robe, and they were told to wait a little longer. (Rev. 6:9–11)

Whether one is on earth or in heaven, the desire for being avenged is a common response to offense and assault. But it still must remain in the hands of the One to whom we belong and to whom vengeance belongs. We pray and He judges. Did you notice that the Lord's response to the wounded ones was to tell them to "wait a little longer"? Patience is mandatory in the reality of handling the offender and the urge to get revenge.

Remember the story in Acts of a bright light knocking Saul off his horse, and his hearing an amazing remark from heaven? "'Saul, Saul, why do you persecute me?' 'Who are you, Lord?' Saul asked. 'I am Jesus, whom you are persecuting,' he replied"

(Acts 9:4–5). The pain Saul was causing God's people was actually causing suffering to Jesus. The offenses I have experienced, so has my Jesus. The offenses my father committed against me, Jesus suffered with me. Because Jesus takes my being offended very personally, I can release revenge, judgment, and payback into His capable hands. God can knock a man off a horse by His very light, His very voice. Imagine what His hands can do!

Sin in Reaction to Sin: Revenge

Revenge is fueled by rage. Anger that ferments and grows can ultimately become rage.

The rape of one's child would obviously result in the experience of rage. The theologian/philosopher Volf, whom I referred to in chapter 3, had this very experience with not just the rape but the murder of his daughter. He had every right to deep, seething rage. Yet he wrote, "We place both our unjust enemy and our own vengeful self face to face with a God who loves and does justice."[8] Volf directs the person in justified rage to consider setting his enemy and himself in God's hands, because only God can handle such rage.

When one woman's daughter was raped at a party, her husband's immediate instinct was to grab his gun and jump in his car to go shoot the kid. Because this father was surrounded by godly men who knew how dangerous revenge is, they helped the father handle the situation with wisdom saturated in God's grace. The mother of this precious girl had been attacked on the way home from school by a group of boys when she was a little girl, so you can see how she could have *easily* desired the death of this boy. But because of Jesus, the revenge gun was never loaded.

Jesus' startling admonition was to pray for those who perse-cute us (see Luke 6:27–28). What could you possibly consider praying for one who has so offended you? There is one prayer I found in Hosea that I pray for people all the time. Now, this type of prayer may seem like a form of revenge, but the results so bless the offender that it isn't revenge. Revenge has no desire for the offender to receive anything but harm.

The prophet Hosea referred to a sort of "blessing of mis-ery." I have prayed this blessing of misery on some who have offended me and for many people I love who are living in abso-lute, stubborn rebellion. Take a look:

I will be like a lion to Ephraim,
   like a great lion to Judah.
I will tear them to pieces and go away;
   I will carry them off, with no one to rescue them.
Then I will go back to my place
   until they admit their guilt.
And they will seek my face;
   in their misery they will earnestly seek me. (Hos. 5:14–15)

What prevents this from being a prayer of revenge is that you are praying for a misery that results in someone's earnestly seeking the Lord. There is no greater blessing on this earth than the passionate pursuit of the Lord. Therefore, asking that God bring people to a place of pursuit, in hopes of a deep heart change (repentance), is an act of mercy rather than revenge.

This verse can actually be read in two different ways. We can pray the blessing of misery on our offenders and hope that in their misery they will finally seek the Lord. Or we can recog-nize in the prophet's words the misery we have already experienced in being offended—the blessing of misery resulting in our own earnestly seeking God.

The depth of insight that comes when a person earnestly seeks God after being harmed by another human being is immeasurable. Isaiah spoke of the power of adversity to change an intellectual understanding into an intimate knowing. It is like watching a master teacher on video who suddenly steps out from behind the screen and imparts insight through his presence as well as his words.

> O people of Zion, who live in Jerusalem, you will weep no more. How gracious he will be when you cry for help! As soon as he hears, he will answer you. Although the Lord gives you the bread of adversity and the water of affliction, your teachers will be hidden no more; with your own eyes you will see them. Whether you turn to the right or to the left, your ears will hear a voice behind you, saying, "This is the way; walk in it." (Isa. 30:19–21)

The Leprous Curse of Vengeance

Through King David we experience a cautionary tale about the pain of avenging oneself:

> When Abner returned to Hebron, Joab took him aside into the gateway, as though to speak with him privately. And there, to avenge the blood of his brother Asahel, Joab stabbed him in the stomach, and he died. Later, when David heard about this, he said, "I and my kingdom are forever innocent before the LORD concerning the blood of Abner son of Ner. May his blood fall upon the head of Joab and upon all his father's house! May Joab's house

never be without someone who has a running sore or lep-
rosy or who leans on a crutch or who falls by the sword or
who lacks food." (2 Sam. 3:27–29)

Joab felt justified in avenging the death of his brother Asahel. Yet this account reveals that revenge is harmful not only to
oneself but also to loved ones. The tragic irony in this story is
that Abner, who was being pursued by Asahel, entreated him
to turn back. Abner did not want to fight Asahel. But young,
stubborn Asahel wanted to fight the big general Abner, and it
resulted in his own death. Joab determined to avenge the death
of a younger brother who was too foolish to turn back when he
was warned. Revenge blinds the avenger and has consequences
reaching far beyond the initial stab in the gut!

Refusing to Join the Vigilante Gang

Vengeance offers short-lived satisfaction but a long-term burden. If I take God's role into my own hands, the burden is more
staggering than the desire to be avenged is satisfied.

I want to review another episode from David's life where,
through a woman named Abigail, this anointed future king of
Israel was kept from joining a vigilante gang out for revenge.
While David was hiding in the wilderness, on the run from
King Saul, he was joined by family and other men who sup-
ported his anointing and future kingship. During that time,
some shepherds with their sheep came into contact with David
and his army and they benefited from his protection. When
the shepherds' owner, Nabal, was asked in turn to be kind and
reward David and his men for their care of his servants and
sheep, Nabal scorned the request (see 1 Sam. 25:14–17).

The Scripture tells us that Nabal was an ill-tempered and difficult man, characteristics boldly displayed in his rude and crude reaction to David's good deeds. In the face of this, David's desire for revenge was understandable. I'm not claiming it was justifiable, but it was understandable. So it is that David's desire for revenge grew as he rehearsed all the good he had done to Nabal and Nabal's subsequent disregard and slanderous reply. Here is David's fuming: "It's been useless—all my watching over this fellow's property in the desert so that nothing of his was missing. He has paid me back evil for good. May God deal with David, be it ever so severely, if by morning I leave alive one male of all who belong to him!" (1 Sam. 25:21–22).

Do you recognize the irony in David's words? He was saying that God should punish him if he *did not* get even with Nabal for this insult. David knew better, but the flame of vengefulness he was fanning into a bonfire was obviously obstructing his good judgment. After all, this was the young man who, as I noted before, restrained himself from revenge in other situations. We should heed David's frame of mind, because we all are susceptible to losing our good judgment when hurt and anger and rehearsing our offenses rile us up into a vengeful froth.

At this point in the story, we discover the courage and wisdom of Abigail. Abigail was Nabal's wife, and, frankly, she is someone from whom we can learn much. By the time Abigail's servants sought her out to tell her all that had transpired, she already stood in that proverbial spot between a rock and a hard place. The Bible tells us that Abigail was entirely aware of her husband's cruel character, and then she had to contend with an infuriated man set on revenge against her whole household because of her husband's wickedness.

Living with a cruel man is emotionally draining, and I believe that the God of Israel must have shown Abigail how to use good judgment rather than resort to excuses when faced with hard decisions and exhausting demands. She did not use her husband's evil dealings as an excuse to hold weekly pity parties. Furthermore, I don't believe Abigail could be labeled as "codependent" on Nabal, because she certainly saw him for what he was. In 1 Samuel 25:25, she said, "May my lord pay no attention to that wicked man Nabal. He is just like his name—his name is Fool, and folly goes with him." In other words, she did not try to explain away Nabal's harsh response to David.

What Abigail did when her servants came to her with the crisis situation (because they knew that you do not present a reasonable request to an unreasonable person, in this case, Nabal) was to wisely move into action. She intercepted David and warned him, and her boldness kept David and four hundred soldiers from killing all the men in her household: "When the LORD has done for my master every good thing he promised concerning him and has appointed him leader over Israel, my master will not have on his conscience the staggering burden of needless bloodshed or of having avenged himself" (1 Sam. 25:30–31).

These are sensible words. These are truthful words. These are the words that brought David back to his right mind. A wise woman kept a man from the *staggering burden of revenge*. Moreover, Abigail reminded David of God's wonderful promises:

> Please forgive your servant's offense, for the LORD will certainly make a lasting dynasty for my master, because he fights the LORD's battles. Let no wrongdoing be found in you as long as you live. Even though someone is pursuing you to take your life, the life of my master will be bound securely in the bundle of the living by the LORD

> your God. But the lives of your enemies he will hurl away
> as from the pocket of a sling. (1 Sam. 25:28–29)

Abigail opened her courageous request for mercy by asking David to forgive the foolish servant who spoke abusively to his men. Abigail understood that forgiving is the only way to defuse revenge. This brave woman reminded the future king that his destiny lay assuredly in the King of kings' hands and that his life was wrapped securely in a bundle—God's treasure pouch. David needed to rest in the reality of God as his Avenger, and Abigail's brilliant reference to David's enemies' being hurled away from the pocket of a sling reminded David that the Lord Almighty was the One who ultimately handled the Goliaths of his life—even if the Goliath was a fool named Nabal.

An anointed earthly king blessed Abigail for her good judgment, and her heavenly King sustained her while married to a fool. Did you know that when the fool died, the earthly king took her as his bride? Yes, Abigail ultimately became David's wife (see v. 40), and David said to her, "May you be blessed for your good judgment and for keeping me from bloodshed" (1 Sam. 25:33).

Again, there is much to learn from the brave and beautiful Abigail. Have you been one to intercept and prevent revenge, or, on the other hand, have you helped fuel the desire for revenge? Even in your own heart, can you recognize that it is the power of forgiveness that defuses the voltage of revenge? Sometimes God uses people as "Abigails" to run interference on revenge, and sometimes the interference comes through His Word. When I wanted to knock out the woman I told you about earlier, God's Word kept me from the staggering burden of revenge, and Abigail's bold example instructed me.

Held Hostage Through Revenge Fantasies

We are often taken captive when we see someone seemingly getting away with offending us. We are impatient because it appears that person is going to escape any retribution for his or her harmful behavior. Revenge fantasies have a tendency to take root when we see the offender happy as a lark and utterly unconcerned about the offense he or she has caused.

I talked to one of my college professors about this: "My offenders don't *look* as if God is disciplining them for harming others." Dr. Porter said, "Jackie, you can't see the miserable insides of a harmful person." I walked away profoundly impacted by that reminder. What people look like in public is often a proud facade that belies the reality of their interior lives.

Scripture instructs,

> Be still before the LORD and wait patiently for him;
>   do not fret when men succeed in their ways,
> when they carry out their wicked schemes.
>   Refrain from anger and turn from wrath;
> do not fret—it leads only to evil.
>   For evil men will be cut off. (Ps. 37:7–9)

I hurt only myself when I fret about the evil that others seem to get away with. I have already been offended, and now I offend myself even deeper by fretting. "Be still" is a wonderful Hebrew phrase that suggests we "slack off."[9] I need to slack off fretting over making people pay for the pain they caused me. I need to take a vacation far away from any revenge fantasy. In fact, the only area of my life in which I want to be known as a "slacker" is in the area of revenge.

Job said, "Have I ever rejoiced when disaster struck my enemies, or become excited when harm came their way? No, I have never sinned by cursing anyone or by asking for revenge" (31:29–30 NLT). When I read this passage, I couldn't help but think that such a forgiving heart is part of the reason God bragged about Job to Satan (see Job 1–2). Effectively, God was boasting about His "lazy" servant, since Job was a true slacker when it came to revenge!

Frisking One's Thoughts

To keep revenge from being a dangerous taskmaster in our lives, we need to frisk our thoughts about the offender pretty regularly. You've seen that the one who offends you, if you do not eventually forgive him or her, will become your master.

What is the only alternative to revenge? This may be painful to hear: it is to pray for the offender. Earlier we saw Jesus' command regarding our offender, even if it is a friend who now seems like an enemy. "Love your enemies; do beautiful good to those hating you; bless those cursing you, and pray over those slandering you" (Luke 6:27–28).[10]

Doesn't revenge seem easier than praying for someone who has slandered you? Shouldn't you be able to do unto the slanderer as he or she did unto you? Shouldn't you be allowed a little gossip and sarcasm when referring to this offensive person—then forgive him or her? Praying for the offender may seem insane, but remaining a slave to past offense is worse. Your flashbacks can be fruitful when prayer, and not a deeper desire for revenge, is the outcome.

A Seemingly Innocent Form of Revenge

The desire to be avenged is so strong that it will try to worm its way into our hearts even when we are trying to frisk every thought and resist revenge fantasies. A typical way that revenge can still infiltrate is when we rejoice that something bad has happened to someone who has harmed us. The Word of God warns us to not break into a cheering chant when something bad happens to our enemy: "Do not gloat when your enemy falls; when he stumbles, do not let your heart rejoice" (Prov. 24:17).

Revenge aborts the reward that I am due because I took matters into my own hands and led a cheering squad when my offender stumbled. I will never forget the comment by a godly woman when she came to my home the day my dad died. She said, "I bet you are relieved that your dad is dead." I was so shocked. She was responding in a very human mentality: "The offender is finally getting what he is due." But my response to my dad's death was utter heartbreak because my dad died having never been born again, and I knew his destiny was hell. No matter how horrible my father was to seven children, I still did not want my dad to go to hell. I had forgiven my dad, and I had prayed that he would repent someday.

The only cure for revenge is to release it into the competent hands of God. Chapter 8 will expound on this activity of doing good to those who offend us, even praying blessings on them to abort our revenge fantasies.

Forgiveness Rather Than Revenge in a Siberian Concentration Camp

More than two decades ago, I read a story that shook me to my core. A Jewish doctor was imprisoned in a Siberian concentration camp, and while he was there, he cared for the sick prisoners with genuine love. Although the men who ran the camp treated him harshly, this doctor never was bitter or even vengeful. In fact, his forgiving lifestyle captured the attention of a young man who had been imprisoned for his political views. The young man was brought to the infirmary with stomach cancer, and this doctor performed surgery that saved his life.

As the young man was recovering from surgery, he would speak with the doctor about his loving attitude toward his harsh captors. This doctor's love for God would not allow him to return evil for evil. One of the prison guards was particularly nasty to the doctor, and this young man was absolutely amazed at the doctor's forgiving attitude. One morning, however, when the young man woke up in the infirmary, he saw the remarkable doctor lying in a pool of his own blood. He would later find out that the guard so hated the doctor, he beat him to death as this young man slept.

As tragic as the situation was, it was not wasted. The suffering of this loving doctor was a life-altering inspiration for the young man who would one day (October 8, 1970) become a Nobel Prize winner—Alexander Solzhenitsyn.[11]

In the same way this Jewish doctor lovingly repaid good for evil to the cruel guards in the Siberian camp, David repaid King Saul good for the evil that King Saul had caused him: "You are a better man than I am, for you have repaid me good for evil" (1 Sam. 24:17 NLT). David never touched God's anointed (he didn't make Saul pay for pursuing David into the wilderness in the hopes of killing him). David's refusing to harm God's chosen king (see 1 Sam. 24:5–6) meant he resisted getting even, and his resistance of revenge produced a "better man." Our obedience in forgiving freely will produce better souls in us. Our obedience will free us to love.

MAKE IT PERSONAL

1. Think about the creative forms of revenge people commonly use: gossip, slander, sarcasm, headaches. When have you seen a loved one use one of these forms? When have you used one? (See Prov. 11:13; 20:19; 18:8.)

2. Can you think of a situation where revenge harmed you more than the one it was intended for? Is revenge a dangerous boomerang? (See Prov. 13:21 NLT; Eph. 4:30, 31.)

3. Does making the offender "pay a little" seem fair to you? Do you make people "squirm" and only then consider forgiving them? (See Lev. 19:17–18; Prov. 24:17; Rom. 12:19.)

4. What emotional battles have you engaged in this year that were fueled by revenge?

5. Is it hard for you even to consider the presence of malice in your heart toward other people? Why? (See Ps. 37:7–9.)

6. How often have you considered the revenge motive behind the sarcasm used incessantly by someone in your life? How is it really "scar-chasm"? (See Luke 6:28.)

7. Have you ever been impatient with God's avenging your heartbreak? How did you handle it (or how are you handling it)? (See Rom. 12:19–21; 2 Thess. 1:6–7.)

8. Read 1 Samuel 25. Have you ever seen an Abigail at work? What did she do? How can you be an Abigail in a conflict you're aware of?

9. Does praying for the one who has slandered you seem preposterous? Why would Jesus ask us to do such a thing? (See Isa. 30:19–21; 40:10; 61:7.)

Chapter 8

Held Hostage by the Incubation of Anger

Excuses for unforgiveness:

1. The offense was too great.
2. The memories of the offense are so vivid.
3. The offense was repeated.
4. You want to make the person pay for the offense.
5. **You are too angry to even consider forgiving this person.**
6. The offender didn't say, "I am sorry."

One of the primary reasons many of us don't forgive is that we're too angry even to consider it. We may or may not be aware of the anger we live with day to day. For plenty of people, the anger that holds them hostage to unforgiveness is a rage stored deep in the attics of their hearts. I refer to this as "ancient anger." Ancient anger is like cobwebs strung across the attics of our hearts, and these cobwebs need to be removed. Frederick Buechner wrote about ancient anger:

> Of the Seven Deadly Sins, anger is possibly the most fun. To lick your wounds, to smack your lips over grievances long past, to roll over your tongue the prospect of bitter confrontations still to come, to savor to the last toothsome morsel both the pain you are given and the pain you are giving back—in many ways it is a feast fit for a king. The chief drawback is that what you are wolfing down is yourself. The skeleton you feast on is you.[1]

It is time to call a cleaning crew to clear out the cobwebs of anger. This cleaning crew can include a pastor, professional counselor, Bible study leader, Sunday school teacher, a prayer partner, or a spiritually mature friend—anyone who will really go in there with you for a thorough cleaning. Let me tell you that if that mass of cobwebs isn't cleaned out, you can pretty much count on the *un*likeliness of becoming free from unforgiveness. The cobwebs of ancient anger will tangle you up!

As we know, the Bible has a lot to say about anger. Does it address ancient anger? Yes, it does! Essentially we are exhorted to not even permit anger to *age*, much less become ancient. A memorable verse that comes to mind when considering the danger of prolonging anger is Ephesians 4:26–27: "'In your anger do not sin': Do not let the sun go down while you are still angry, and do not give the devil a foothold."

I used to think "foothold" meant something like a foot caught in the door, and, frankly, that never bothered me. I thought, *Oh, yeah, I'm scared—squish the devil—his foot is in the door.* Then a speaker who heard me joke about the foothold challenged me to look a little closer at the word. The King James translation of the verse says, "Neither give place to the devil." "Place" is far more intimidating to me than "foothold." As I examined the word *place*, I discovered this definition: "a location, condition, opportunity."[2]

Yikes! I didn't realize that a *foothold* offers an opportunity as well as the suitable condition for anger to dwell. Then I thought about Satan's influence in my life. *Wait a minute. The Holy Ghost comes in when I'm born again, so the Holy Ghost is not going to allow the enemy of my soul to make a dwelling or a location within me.* Yet the word *location* can also mean a vicinity of my life where Satan has been given a degree of influence. He's influencing me through my untamed anger.

Imagine driving home from church on Sunday, and suddenly you notice that someone has set up a campsite on your front lawn—tent, campfire, and all. This person is not actually inside your house, but he is on your lawn—he is camped on your property. The enemy of our souls shows up when we get angry, sets up housekeeping out on the front lawn, and then traps us through our angry, unforgiving hearts.

I finally grasped that my unforgiving heart, fueled by anger, was a place of influence and camping out for the enemy. Do you see that if we allow the sun to set on our anger, the camp crew just returns under cover of darkness? From that point, the devil's inclination is to see how far he can push: "If I could just get a foot in the door...." Anger without a time limit on it just helps Satan get a foot in the door of our lives. No thank you!

Danger of Anger After Sunset

When I was in college, I was impressed with the relationship between my English literature teacher (Dr. Evangeline Banta) and her husband. She invited me to spend a weekend at her home, where I got a closer look at a love relationship that I had assumed existed only in literature. At the end of our weekend together, I asked Evangeline what was the secret of the love that had flourished after forty-plus years of marriage. I've never forgotten her remark, and it has been the most important marital advice I've ever received. Evangeline said, "We made a commitment on our wedding night that we would not go to sleep angry with one another." Such a simple remark, but it is a foundational truth for love that will last a lifetime. Going to bed angry with one's mate will only result in dragon breath come morning.

Paul described the marriage relationship as a reflection of the heavenly Bridegroom and His earthly bride. To the husbands he said, "Love your wives, just as Christ loved the church.... This is a great mystery, but it is an illustration of the way Christ and the church are one" (Eph. 5:25, 32 NLT). I used to cringe when I heard of the symbol of marriage compared with Christ and His church, since so many marriages are in such pitiful condition today. Then I realized that the emotional divorce that exists within many marriages is due to unresolved conflict (too many nights going to bed angry). It is the same emotional divorce I see between Christ and His church. Many Christians are divorced from true intimacy with God because they have grieved and quenched the Holy Spirit (see Eph. 4:30; 1 Thess. 5:19). The Holy Spirit is grieved when we do not willingly put away anger and bitterness; likewise, our marriage relationships experience the same gaps and grief when we do not deal with our anger and bitterness. Just as Christians can choose to live with a gap between God and themselves, many couples choose to live day in and day out with gaps as wide as the English Channel.

At my bridal shower, married women were encouraged to give me advice, and my hostess recorded it for me. Every married woman gave her version of the advice that Evangeline gave me that weekend. One woman challenged me to be the first one to make the move across the emotional Grand Canyon caused by conflict. Men are uncomfortable with emotional realities and need marriage to teach them about handling anger before the sun sets daily. This same woman said that the first move in resolving conflict is the most difficult, but once the first step is taken, one senses the ability to sprint into the rest of the process.

An Unresolved Rage Can Have Fatal Consequences

As I have said in these pages, I forgave my father for abusing me and some of my other siblings. I was impacted by their abuse as well as mine; we were all impacted by one another's pain. At my father's funeral one of my favorite counselors asked me after the service, "Has your brother ever talked to anybody about what your dad did to you guys?" I said, "Oh, no. Johnny's an introvert. He keeps his feelings bottled up inside." I told the counselor that when my sister killed herself four years earlier, Johnny was driving me to the airport and I implored him to go talk to someone. His sharp response was, "About what! About Dad? That's got nothing to do with now, that's yesterday! I'm married, and that is the past." Soft-spoken Johnny had revealed his bottled-up anger.

When I finished sharing this, the counselor looked at me and said, "If he doesn't deal with that bottled-up rage, he could be the next one!" I remember staring back at him with tears streaming down my face, saying, "Don't even say things like that!"

Three years later, when my brother did kill himself and the police came to tell me, I screamed in agony. The first thing out of my mouth was, "Dad killed another one!" As my husband drove me to tell my mom, I kept thinking in anguished sarcasm, *No, Johnny, you didn't need counseling, you didn't need to forgive Dad. Isn't that why you took your life?* Instead of dealing with it, he shoved the pain down deep in his heart, and one day it surfaced in the form of a gun placed to his head in a hotel room.

Anger's Camouflage

Before we go further, let's make sure we are aware of the ways that anger is manifested. Here is a little reality check: *all hurt is followed by the secondary emotion of anger.* Some think anger is simply yelling or cursing, but it can become apparent in many other ways:

Criticism
Silence
Sulking
Sarcasm
Intimidation
Hypochondria
Depression
Petty complaints
Gossip
Stubbornness
Halfhearted efforts (passive-aggressive)
Forgetfulness
Procrastination

Laziness
Numbness
Compulsive behaviors (excessive eating, shopping, working)

Furthermore, we have come to know a lot about the physical symptoms of swallowed anger. A higher susceptibility to serious illnesses, such as heart disease and cancer, can be traced to stuffing anger.[3] Yet, regrettably, whenever you go to the doctor, and he wants information on your family's medical history, he will ask about only heart disease, cancer, or diabetes; I have never seen "anger" on the medical form. My father died from congestive heart failure, and I believe that the specific root of all his physical complications could be traced to the raging anger that pulsed throughout his life.

Scripture says, "Do not make friends with a hot-tempered man, do not associate with one easily angered, or you may learn his ways and get yourself ensnared" (Prov. 22:24–25). But I never had a choice about living with a hot-tempered father. I never had a choice about associating with a huge clan of easily angered people. Family get-togethers were always occasions for big fights. One Thanksgiving, arguing broke out during dinner, and one by one my brothers and sisters and their families left. When the noise subsided, my husband was the only one left eating at the table.

When I became a Christian, I realized that I had a snare in my soul and I would often cry, asking Jesus to remove my propensity for anger. I came to realize I had a choice not only in relation to being angry, but also in associating with other people and their anger. After years of studying and soul-searching, I have learned how to manage my proclivity toward anger. The Holy Spirit has taught me that I can be angry and not sin—just repent and forgive before sunset! The Holy Spirit also gives me the power to not harm myself or others with the anger I sometimes experience. "Better a patient man than a warrior, a man who controls his temper than one who takes a city" (Prov. 16:32).

Let me emphasize that controlling anger is *not* merely pushing it underground. What looks like self-control will only manifest later in bitterness and/or depression. When we cover over our anger, guess what happens? We get compounded interest. For me, what went in as anger came forth as rage. When I got hurt as a kid, it went underground as anger and when it came forth later in life, it became a monster.

When Was the Incubator Turned On?

Throughout the years, I have observed that a great number of Christians are in absolute denial about the anger in their hearts. They believe anger is not acceptable in a follower of Jesus. This misconception must be corrected before we go any further. If you believe that the very experience of anger is sinful, then God has sinned. Have you ever considered the number of references in the Old Testament that contain God and anger in the same sentence? I have heard many speakers refer to hundreds of verses in the Bible that mention anger, and the majority of verses refer to God's anger. Look at just one example: "Nothing will remain but to cringe.... Yet for all this, his [God's] anger is not turned away, his hand is still upraised" (Isa. 10:4).

If anger is a sinless emotion, how does it become sin? It becomes sin through incubation. In response to disappointment, our emotions can progress from hurt to anger to resentment to bitterness. Anger does not stay in one place. It is moving and growing, and it is not moving in a positive direction. This is what I call the "incubation of anger."

An incubator is a machine that maintains favorable conditions for growth and development. It is used to nurture everything from premature babies to chicks. In contrast to these positive uses of incubation, we also know that germs and disease can be cultivated in an incubator. And in terms of our anger, a conducive environment for incubation will include grudge books, revenge fantasies, self-pity, pride, and the sun going down while we are still angry.

Sadly, another element that supports this incubation of anger is the denial of anger. The very thing that we Christians imagine protects us from "sinning" by feeling anger is what actually encourages its successful incubation—denial and the camouflaging of anger. If you look again at that list of anger's camouflaged manifestations, you see that depression, procrastination, hypochondria, passive aggression, sarcasm, and so forth are actually the outcomes of anger being incubated in our hearts. When you are offended, you are often disappointed, and that disappointment moves into the secondary emotion of anger. When someone you love disappoints you, you must resist turning the incubator on and allowing your disappointment to grow into anger.

God is all about our venting the wrong to Him. If you notice while you are getting ready to go to sleep that you still have anger free-floating in your heart, it is vent-to-God time. King David recommended it: "In your anger do not sin; when you are on your beds, search your hearts and be silent. Offer right sacrifices and trust in the LORD" (Ps. 4:4–5).

As you examine your heart, searching for any anger, keep in mind that God wants you to trust Him with the disappointment, offense, and heartache. When you choose to trust Him with your disappointment, the anger will begin to subside. Trust is a great remedy for anger. After your venting, ask God's forgiveness for cultivating anger from emotion to sin by letting it incubate in your heart.

For several years, whenever I would read about Moses' anger and the consequence of being deprived of entering the Promised Land, I would grieve that my anger, like Moses', would cost me the Promised Land (I don't mean heaven, but my inheritance in Jesus). This year, when I read through this passage, I saw that Moses' anger was a symptom of his lack of trust: "This is because both of you broke faith with me in the presence of the Israelites" (Deut. 32:51).

I had felt sorry for Moses, because I felt his frustration with a rebellious group of people was justified. After all, Moses was frustrated with a people who could actually doubt after witnessing the parting of the Red Sea! Then God showed me that even Moses, a man of great faith (see Heb.11:23–29), struggled with trusting God, and this was manifested through his anger. Whenever I am angry, I consider not only the person or circumstance but also the extent that I am not trusting God. I do not want my tombstone to be located in Moab (see Deut. 34:1, 5–6).

PhD Insight on Anger — Owning My Anger Toward God

Learning to trust God with my ancient anger has been extremely challenging. It took a gifted and insightful man to recognize profound anger creating an entire wall of cobwebs in my heart's attic. I was shocked the day that he sat down across from me, looked me straight in the eye, and said, "Jackie, now tell me when you finally settled your anger toward God."

"What?" I exclaimed. "I'm not mad at God! I am mad at my dad. I am mad at my mother for staying with my dad. I was mad at a society that made me feel so much shame even as a victim that I couldn't even confide in a pastor in a church—"

But he interrupted, saying, "Hold it, who let that happen?"

I thought, *God.*

He then said to me, "Okay, Jackie, it's time to do business with the fact that you're ultimately mad at God."

This was an idea I had never encountered before. "Oh, no, I'm not mad at God. I love God."

He said, "Jackie, you love your husband. Have you ever been mad at him?"

"Of course, many times."

"Well, if you love your husband and you can be mad at him, so you can love God and be mad at Him."

So on December 9, 1990, Bob Gilmore and several others at Palm Bible Chapel laid hands on me and said, "It's time to do business." Tears poured down my face as I said to the Lord, "O Father God, I never realized that I needed to ask Your forgiveness because You're the One I'm maddest at. You're the One who gave me this family I didn't sign up for." That day was a major turning point for me. I no longer have God on trial; He's not on the stand anymore. I fully trust Him to bring good out of the horror of my childhood.

Think about your typical response to being offended. Is it lashing out? Is it the silent treatment—sulking, pouting, and staring off into the sunset? Is it spouting off sarcastically? Do you have an angry larynx—smoldering anger revealing itself in slander, gossip, and criticism? James recommended, "Let every man be swift to hear, slow to speak, slow to wrath; for the wrath of man does not produce the righteousness of God" (James 1:19–20 NKJV).

Let's look at some typical responses to being offended.

Lashing Out

Ever have a simple discussion that turned into a heated argument? You wondered, *What was that about?!* Have you ever said something hateful and your immediate thought was *Where did that come from?* Often enough, such harsh remarks and argumentative statements are stimulated by unaddressed anger. As Jesus said, "Out of the overflow of the heart the mouth speaks" (Matt. 12:34).

In Luke 2:49, the young boy Jesus made some remarks that His mother did not understand, and she pondered them in her heart for years (2:50–51). Apparently they were words of such deep wisdom that she would not comprehend them until Jesus grew up. By contrast, as a child I also heard remarks that I did not understand, and I, too, pondered them in my heart for years. But these remarks were hardly full of wisdom. They were very cruel and deeply painful. Now, as an adult, I understand the impact of the harsh words I heard so regularly. My heart's overflow is too often a painful reminder of what I stored there years ago. Such anger in my young heart helped create an argumentative teenager and young adult.

Only in the last ten years have I understood the correlation between my angry remarks and an "ailing" (sick) heart. Job 16:3 says, "What ails you that you keep on arguing?" The word translated "ailing" is in Hebrew a word that means "pressed to pungent, to irritate."[4] Talk about a searchlight being turned on in my soul. Suddenly I understood the source of my own angry overflow: past hurt feelings of abuse, injustice, criticism, and rejection. All of these had been pressing on my heart, and the overflow had been pungent. Years of stored feelings of pain fermented into a very angry, sick heart.

By God's grace, I have been given the strength to look at the issues that poisoned me for years. As I keep forgiving people who contributed to the pungent overflow, my ailing heart is getting better, and my angry mouth and argumentative attitude are becoming more of a distant memory than a daily occurrence.

The next time you are with an argumentative person, pray for insight into the things that are pressing on his or her heart and causing an angry overflow. The past is not an excuse for our present anger, but it can give us valuable clues for dealing with the pungent storage that is a constant fuel line to an angry, argumentative attitude. Knowing what is in the storage areas of our hearts allows us to confront those things that supply the crushing remarks, which spill out of an ailing heart through angry lips.

Sulking

Another response to offense, seemingly the opposite of lashing out, is sulking. If sulking silence is how you react to being offended, think about this: withdrawing into silence is not just a defense mechanism but a subtle way of making the other person pay. Sulking and pouting can be a form of revenge—payback. When your spouse or a friend hurts you and you just close up, look out the window, and stare, you're getting compounded interest on that anger. The longer it stays under, the more anger grows—so much so that when you explain it to the person who hurt you, he or she will stare at you in bewilderment because it has grown into a separate beast. "He who conceals his hatred has lying lips, and whoever spreads slander is a fool" (Prov. 10:18). Anger pushed underground through sulking or pouting may rupture later in slander and gossip.

I cannot state this strongly enough. Living in unforgiving anger is such a waste of your precious life. God's Word encourages us to release the anger and stop rehearsing the hurt. Here is what some experts say:

> According to Dr. Luskin [who conducted the Stanford Forgiveness Project], we go through four stages in learning to forgive. To begin with, we focus on what others are doing to us. We blame outside people and situations for what happens, and do not see that the anger response is a choice we are making. In the second stage, we turn our focus on what we are doing to ourselves. We realize that anger does not "feel good," and take steps to release it and forgive. In the third stage, we start to notice our anger responses even to simple everyday situations, "such as being cut off by another car on the expressway." We become aware of anger's discomfort, and realize that the length of time we spend in this state is a choice we can make. In stage four, Luskin says, "We have realized that not only is anger uncomfortable and a waste of 'precious life,' it is something that hurts other people. At this stage, we decide to stop reacting to life with anger."[5]

The Abortion of Love in Any Relationship

Years ago I was studying the impact of anger on love relationships, and I found this verse: "Thus saith the LORD; For three transgressions of Edom, and for four, I will not turn away the punishment thereof; because he did pursue his brother with the sword, and did cast off all pity, and his anger did tear perpetually, and he kept his wrath for ever" (Amos 1:11 KJV).

As I examined the behavior that God was not willing to overlook, I was awestruck.

> Because he did pursue his brother with the sword,
> and did cast off all pity [*pity:* compassion, as cherishing a fetus]
> and his anger did tear [*tear:* pluck off, tear to pieces] perpetually
> and he kept [*kept:* built hedge around to guard it] his wrath forever.[6]

The fact is, *anger aborts love; forgiveness aborts anger and frees me to love.*

I know the word *aborts* seems harsh, but the destructive path of protected anger is just that dangerous. My unchecked anger is like giving Satan the combination of the lock on my heart's treasures.

My husband, Ken, and I watched the movie *Walk the Line*, based on the life of Johnny Cash. During the movie there were several painful scenes between Johnny Cash and his father. Johnny's father was a merciless perfectionist, and his incessant criticism of Johnny helped fuel years of addiction. The shame and anger caused in the heart of a child who has been exasperated by a perfectionistic parent is seen not only in the life of Johnny Cash but in the lives of millions who have heart wounds from such unloving parents. After the movie Ken said, "I was raised by two perfectionists, and I am a perfectionist, and I am concerned about the impact on our children. I want to ask them three questions when I get home: What do I do or say that discourages you? Do I do anything or say anything that encourages you? What would you like me to do or say that would encourage you?"

Ken asked both our children, and neither had any major complaints. My heart was touched that Ken was sensitive enough to want to ask such questions. Most parents are often clueless concerning the exasperation and hurt that they have caused their children despite Paul's admonition: "Fathers, do not exasperate your children; instead, bring them up in the training and instruction of the Lord" (Eph. 6:4).

If you have struggled with shame and anger and you haven't been able to trace the source, maybe you need to consider the impact of a parent's words on your heart as a child. A therapist told me, "Jackie, verbal abuse causes heart wounds just like sexual abuse does." How shocked most critical parents are when they discover the destructive damage done by their criticism and perfectionism. By the same token, silent and neglectful parents can wound as well—another method of aborted love through anger.

I have seen parents who are passionately committed to their children's academics and sports participation, but who apparently did not invest even a moment in instructing their children on handling conflict with one another. Fighting that is not followed by forgiveness only allows the anger to fester underground, and the fighting will continue at a future date. Teaching children how to forgive and ask forgiveness should be on the to-do list of every parent. "Pleasant words are a honeycomb, sweet to the soul and healing to the bones" (Prov. 16:24).

It can seem impossible to be objective about our issues with anger because of the unspoken taboo concerning anger in the life of any loving Christian. However, an accurate view of anger in our lives can work like a security system, warning us of the possible presence of unforgiveness, which inevitably stifles love in one's life. We think it is anger that kills love when, in fact, it is unforgiveness intensifying anger that ultimately destroys the love between people. Therefore, let's be courageous and persistent in acknowledging anger and chasing down its source in our hearts and minds.

To help you gauge your own methods of dealing with anger, I've made the "Make It Personal" question list a bit longer in this chapter. See where you need to improve — and begin today. Don't let anger and a drive for revenge keep you from the freedom to forgive — and to love.

MAKE IT PERSONAL

1. Do you carefully validate your facts before blasting someone? Give an example.
2. Do you frequently check for the possibility of displaced anger (you're angry at your boss, so you kick your dog)? How can you begin to do this habitually? (See Eph. 4:26, 27; Prov. 16:32.)
3. Are you comfortable with telling God how angry you are? Tell Him something that angered you today. (See Ps. 4:4, 5.)
4. Do you freely confess when your anger results in sin — when it harms your relationship with another? Why or why not? (See Prov. 22:24–25; James 1:19–20.)
5. Can you remember any speeches you regret? Words spoken

in anger are words always regretted (see Prov. 10:19). Describe one of these speeches.

6. Do you procrastinate when dealing with anger? How do you do this? Remember, anger not dealt with, after many sunsets, results in emotional divorce.

7. Do you tend to withdraw into silence when angry with someone? What would be a healthier response to your anger? (See Prov. 10:18.)

8. Do you often dredge up past issues during present-tense anger? Remember to keep short accounts.

9. Can you express your expectations honestly without sulking? Give an example of doing this.

10. Can you express your hurt/complaint in a calm tone of voice? Why or why not?

11. Do you express your complaint against someone to him or her privately? Public confrontation is shaming and fuels more anger.

12. Do you value maintaining relationships more than winning arguments? How do you know this is true? (See Job 16:3.)

13. When you are angry, do you resist resorting to threats? Is this part of your parenting technique? If you are tempted to make threats, how can you begin to change this habit? (See Eph. 6:4; Prov. 16:24.)

14. Do you succumb to name-calling? Attack the problem, not the person.

15. Do you resist exaggeration? This can escalate into major war.

16. Do you actively look for solutions to conflict?

17. Do you understand what your style is during conflict? Do you attack or withdraw? Are you a shark or a turtle?

Part III

Escape for Hostages Who Want to Be Free

Chapter 9

Forgiveness Tool of Praying Blessings on the Offender

A s we have considered different excuses people use to avoid forgiving, we have seen examples of what our flesh manufactures to protect our vulnerable selves. No matter how much we like to imagine otherwise, these are not effective methods to bring freedom. What we really need are tools that engineer liberty for our hearts, that sever and demolish the lies that bind us and keep us imprisoned by unforgiveness. We need tools that fashion forgiveness.

Here is a remarkable thought: every excuse for unforgiveness actually comprises some invaluable material. How amazing that our infinitely wise Father God calls us to forgive and then coaches us to take what our flesh manufactures and place it in His capable hands. There a miracle takes place: excuses that once bound us become the very material for tools that liberate us from being held hostage to yesterday. This transformation takes place in the same way that one forgives—by faith.

This chapter will cover the molding of a specific excuse into a tool. The last two chapters will address the transformation of

all the excuses into tools that the believer has had access to all
the time!

Waiting for Three Words: "I Am Sorry"

Too often we think we have forgiven people in the past because
we have forgotten the offenses. This isn't always true. What we
often think was forgotten may actually have imbedded itself as
part of our relationship style, and we don't even recognize it. A
young woman I met constantly said, "I don't like to get close to
other women. They are so catty!" This young woman distanced
herself from the women who had hurt her—and essentially
from all women. This choice was not forgiveness, and the unforgiveness has impacted her relational style with women to this
day. Remember, hurt that is buried is resurrected in another
form that is not helpful.

Excuses for unforgiveness:
1. The offense was too great.
2. The memories of the offense are so vivid.
3. The offense was repeated.
4. You want to make the person pay for the offense.
5. You are too angry to even consider forgiving this person.
6. The offender didn't say, "I am sorry."

A common misunderstanding about forgiving others is tied
up in three little words: "I am sorry." Waiting for these words
can keep a person locked in the prison of unforgiveness for
years!

One of my friends told me, "What keeps me from forgiving
someone boils down to one thing: I want them to admit they're

at fault!" Do you relate to these words? I have met thousands of people who are stuck in unforgiveness, not because the offense was mortal but because their offenders haven't said they're sorry—yet. They're waiting for the offenders to come to their senses and ask for forgiveness. If the perpetrator in your life does do this—great! Yet what will you do, day to day, until that moment? This chapter will help you stop waiting for those words and move you to living in freedom whether your offender ever apologizes or not.

I received an e-mail from a girl the other day whose dad had abused her. He is getting counseling for his predatory behavior, and he has finally asked for her forgiveness. That's extraordinary, but that's *reconciliation*. Reconciliation, as I described in chapter 4, occurs when the offended hears those three words, "I am sorry," accepts the apology, and the relationship is restored. (Note, however, that reconciliation is not always a healthy step. Sometimes you need to leave your abuser behind and forget ever having a relationship with him or her, because he or she will continue to hurt you in one way or another.)

What about the rest of the kids in America who have fathers who will never repent, who will never own what they did? Are they doomed to live in unforgiveness? Must those who are waiting for "I am sorry" stay in prison? No. You need to be released from prison before you ever hear the words "I am sorry"! Let's get this really clear: forgiveness can exist without reconciliation.

I have heard people say, "I'm not going to forgive them until they say they're sorry, until they crawl across glass and beg forgiveness. When they bleed, I'll forgive them." Do you see how that changes forgiveness from a gift given to something earned? Demanding an apology before forgiving is requiring people to *earn* your forgiveness. And here's another important point: even if you effectively communicate to someone how he or she has offended you and you get the person to apologize, if it is done begrudgingly and not sincerely, you will not be satisfied. Consequently, how do you live without the three words that will free your heart?

An Irresistible Example of Forgiveness

An earth-shattering moment on the cross applies so perfectly to our longing to hear "I am sorry." Jesus gave us the example of forgiving His offenders who had not remotely acknowledged their need to say "I'm sorry": "Jesus said, 'Father, forgive them, for they do not know what they are doing'" (Luke 23:34).

You are already thinking, *But that is Jesus, not me*. You may also be thinking, *I know that the one who offended me knew what he was doing*. As I mentioned earlier, though, much of the time offenders are clueless wonders—totally blind to the wounds they are causing. Most people who have offended us don't even know they've done it. They go through their days offending people and go to sleep totally unaware of the wounded lying all around them.

Remember James 3:2: "In many things we offend all" (KJV). The Jerusalem Bible (Doubleday, 1966) translates this verse: "After all, every one of us does something wrong, over and over again." Talk about a sobering translation: the reality is that we all offend in many ways, and we offend again and again.

How can people be so careless with their remarks, even among those they are close to emotionally? Again, if a person has a pulse, he has a chance of offending you and being clueless—and never giving you those vital three words, "I am sorry."

I have tried to follow Jesus' example of forgiving my offenders even when they haven't said they are sorry, because that is how Jesus handled the soldiers who crucified Him. Jesus forgave the Roman soldiers as they gambled for His clothes and mocked Him on the cross. When you and I refuse to forgive, we are simply giving in to the temptation of unforgiveness and vengeance. When you and I forgive those who haven't apologized, we are protecting ourselves from the inevitability of bitterness. In his book *The Resilient Life,* Gordon MacDonald has a wonderful grasp on this fresh look at Luke 23:34:

> He [Jesus] was aware that forgiving his enemies was a pro-active defense against any temptation to become embittered toward them. . . . If we embrace the truth that Jesus was fully God and fully man and thus capable of facing all temptations (as is said in the book of Hebrews), then I think we're watching a Savior who is protecting Himself against the temptation of hatred and resentment.[1]

What Jesus offers us in this prayer is a profound thing. This is the forgiveness tool of praying for our offenders. The excuse not to forgive until one hears the infamous three words can be transformed into this tool of calling down blessings upon those who hurt us; and when I employ this tool, I am not only forgiving but actively resisting the temptation to not forgive. Yahoo!

Let's look at how such a transformation can take place. How does one take the excuse of "He didn't say, 'I'm sorry,'" and transform it into the faith-filled gesture of praying blessings on one's offender? (By the way, as you have read through this book, how many offenders have come to your mind? Take heart! You are on the verge of ultimate freedom.)

Job's Empowerment

If we look again at the book of Job, we find a situation in which a victim is in the place of power. The victim himself is asked to pray for his offensive friends, and Job's forgiving prayer is more powerful than the sacrifices his friends were offering for their sins:

> After the LORD had finished speaking to Job, he said to Eliphaz the Temanite: "I am angry with you and your two friends, for you have not spoken accurately about me, as my servant Job has. So take seven bulls and seven rams and go to my servant Job and offer a burnt offering for yourselves. My servant Job will pray for you, and I will accept his prayer on your behalf. *I will not treat you as you deserve.*" (Job 42:7–8 NLT, emphasis added)

How ironic that Job's friends were forgiven their repetitive, slanderous, cruel remarks through the compassionate, forgiving prayer of Job. *The victim actually became the vessel for forgiveness.* Read these verses and realize that *the victim stands in the most powerful place in relation to the offender not when he responds in revenge, but when he forgives.* This is the key to transforming the excuse into a powerful forgiving tool.

You will recall when the Lord showed me how to overcome evil with good by purchasing a gift for my slanderous offender. Well, that method of blessing others with gifts was becoming pretty costly. So I wouldn't end up in bankruptcy, God gave me additional instruction in resisting revenge and overcoming evil with good. Indeed, what He gave me was "the most excellent way" (1 Cor. 12:31). He showed me how to respond to offense through praying blessings on the offender. I was not only willing to relinquish my right to hurt the one who hurt me, but I fortified this relinquishment by praying a blessing on him or her.

Those who are familiar with the book of Job know that he went through a terrible time in which God permitted unspeakable levels of pain. The suffering was compounded when three of Job's friends showed up. They sat with Job in silent commiseration for seven days, and then—they opened their mouths. The things they said were like salt applied to an open wound.

But in the end, God showed His disapproval of the friends' counsel. He told Job that his friends not only had to bring bulls and rams as sin offerings, but they had to be prayed for by *the one they offended*. After the one who was offended prayed a blessing over his friends, then God would expedite mercy ("I will not treat you as you deserve").

Until then, bulls and rams were sufficient sin offerings, based on the law in Leviticus. But in Job God added to the process by asking the one offended to pray a blessing on the offenders. Do you hear it? God had taken an unforgiving situation of verbal offense and transformed it into a banner day of victory for the offenders! God said to Job, "Job, I need you to release a blessing on them that they don't deserve."

Victim in the Place of Power

Here is a situation in which a victim was placed in the position of power. The victim was asked to pray for his offensive friends, and Job's forgiving prayer was more powerful than the sacrifices his friends were offering for their sins.

Let's get our minds around this. This is true irony, but utterly characteristic of our Lord. *A victim stands in the most powerful place of forgiveness when he offers a prayer on behalf of the offender.* The victim actually becomes the vessel for forgiveness. This happens not when one responds in revenge but when one forgives. Like an earthquake, these verses shook my world as a forgiver. The Rock of Ages rocked me to the core.

I realized through this teaching from God that instead of purchasing gifts for my offenders, I can call down blessings—God's favor—treatment beyond what the offenders deserve. This is far greater than any material gift I could give them. Praying blessings on those who may never say they are sorry transforms my excuse into a forgiveness tool.

How to Use the Forgiveness Tool of Praying Blessings

Mahatma Gandhi said, "The weak can never forgive. Forgiveness is an attribute of the strong." If you can call down divine favor on behalf of someone who doesn't deserve it, you will have your finest hour. Remember, I am like Jesus not when I am perfect, but when I am forgiving. James wrote, "Whatever you say or whatever you do, remember that you will be judged by the law [of love] that sets you free" (James 2:12 NLT).

When I speak a blessing in prayer over my offender, I am doing nothing less than fulfilling the "law of love." This law of love was the foundation of our own forgiveness, and when we forgive others we are liberating ourselves to live the law of love. Our excuses, on the other hand, nullify the law of love.

The forgiveness tool of praying a blessing on offenders is something you can use throughout the day, whether at work, in the middle of a lunch appointment, or walking down the aisle of the grocery store. This tool is quicker than text messaging. It can be a flash prayer sent to God in the moment of offense or in a sudden memory of the offense.

How do you know what to pray for the offender? To use this forgiveness tool most effectively, before you can pray a blessing on another, you need to pray for wisdom. Ask God what you should pray. You may be wondering, *How will I know the answer is from God?* The holy nudge will come in the form of an idea that benefits the other person. Remember, God told Job to pray that God would treat his friends better than they deserved. Job prayed a merciful blessing upon his offending friends. God was the tutor for Job's praying blessing on his friends, and God wants to be your tutor as you apprentice in using this potent forgiveness tool. James wrote, "If any of you lacks wisdom, he should ask God, who gives generously to all without finding fault, and it will be given to him" (James 1:5).

When you and I honestly admit our excuses and ask for wisdom to pray blessings upon those who have hurt us, we can be confident in God's provision, because He is the initiator of all forgiveness. God wants to help us resist the temptation of unforgiveness that simply carries too high a price tag for us.

Years ago, after a woman heard me teach on forgiveness she came up to me and said, "I am so angry with you about this 'pray blessings' instruction." I appreciated her candor, and I asked what made her angry.

She yelled, "You expect me to pray a blessing on my husband, who ran off with my friend and committed adultery!" As calmly as I could I said, "If you want to be free, you have to forgive your husband." She responded, "I can't do that blessing part! I'll do the forgiving." She argued with me for a few more minutes, and I did the best I could to explain to her that praying a blessing on her ex-husband was a forgiveness tool that would fortify her desire to let go of her rage about his betrayal.

Knowing I would see her the next week, I said, "I dare you to get in your car and before you turn the motor on—ask God to drop into your mind and heart a blessing you could pray for your ex-husband."

The next week when I saw her, she was beaming. I knew in my heart she had asked for wisdom and that God had creatively given her a blessing for her offender. She told me her story. The week prior, she was still so angry at my suggestion that she sat in her car mentally battling the notion of asking God to give her something to pray over the husband who left her. She slammed the door, put on her seat belt, and all of a sudden, a thought went through her mind: *Pray for reconciliation between your ex-husband and his son.* She was shocked by this suggestion. Her ex-husband had a child who had not spoken to him in years. Praying for their reconciliation would be a miraculous blessing. So, sitting in her car, she prayed this blessing over her former husband. The moment she prayed the prayer, she said she felt as if a heavy pack had fallen off her back.

She was not only delighted that the burden had been lifted, she was thrilled that she had learned how to use the forgiveness tool of praying a blessing. Using this forgiveness tool is a mature act, as it displays obedience to the law of love—forgiving freely as one has been forgiven. What was done *to* us will be healed by what was done *for* us.

This woman's relief was immediate, but for some, the relief is not an instantaneous experience. Many people have told me that it has taken several prayers of blessings before the relief began to seep into their souls. Even when people experience relief, they will use the forgiveness tool again in the future—whether facing a memory of the offense or facing a new offense committed by the offender.

Her prayer may have begun in disbelief, but how God responded strengthened her faith. We are called to live by faith, and we forgive by faith also. This forgiveness tool is utilized by faith. Utilizing this prayer blessing tool helps fortify our desire to forgive and forgive again.

Bonus Gift for the Aggressive Forgiver

Praying blessings on the offender wasn't the only gift God gave me that day so long ago. In the verse following, there is a gift for the forgiver. This transformation of the excuse into a forgiving tool has an embedded bonus. What could be more wonderful than being liberated from bondage to my offender and having the burden of unforgiveness fall off my back? Look at Job 42:10 in three different Bible versions:

> After Job had prayed for his friends, the LORD made him prosperous again. (NIV)

> The LORD turned the captivity of Job, when he prayed for his friends. (KJV)

> After Job had interceded for his friends, GOD restored his fortune—and then doubled it! (THE MESSAGE)

As you can see, after Job's prayerful gesture of forgiveness, the Lord made him prosperous again, turned his captivity, and restored—and doubled—his fortune.

Whatever the translation, the reality is that Job's usage of the forgiveness tool of praying a blessing over his offenders resulted in an incredible blessing from God. Job's prayer for his foolish friends liberated them from God's wrath over their folly. Furthermore, it liberated Job from the bitter captivity of a major life crisis, as well as the resulting insult and injury from "good friends."

If you have been hesitant to pray for your offender(s), don't remain in captivity one more moment. Ask God to give you a blessing you can call down on your offender. One of the blessings you can always pray is that the offender will ask God's forgiveness for his or her offensive behavior. You can always ask God to bless the offender with the soul care he or she needs.

Do you have a fortune that needs restoring? I don't necessarily mean a material fortune, although it is true that God blesses people in material ways. But what about an abundance of peace or contentment that has been squandered throughout your season of resentment? Are you in a captive situation from which you need release? Well, whom haven't you prayed a blessing on? Toward what person are you harboring unforgiveness? If you have been clamoring for peace when you haven't prayed the blessing yet on your offender, you are holding up your own restoration and blessings.

I can't even conceive how many rewards I have cheated myself out of because I was too busy trying to get even instead of utilizing the forgiveness tool of praying blessings on my offender. God asks us to be kind to our enemies, not because it is His idea of a cruel joke, but because it is a chance to experience daily the wonders of forgiveness freely given. While we were enemies of God, Jesus willingly died for us (see Rom. 5:8). Let's not forget: "If, when we were God's enemies, we were reconciled to him through the death of his Son, how much more, having been reconciled, shall we be saved through his life!" (Rom. 5:10).

What a holy paradox: we are blessed most when we release a blessing on our offenders. I can only imagine how many Christians have been waiting on the blessing of the Lord, waiting for the day of deliverance, waiting to get out of the rut they're in, waiting to get out of the terrible dark season—and they have never even considered that they themselves have prolonged the time of great struggle through unforgiveness.

Resisting My Own Blessing Potential

We actually can risk blocking blessings with our names on them when we stubbornly refuse to pray blessings upon those who have offended us. The apostle Peter wrote, "Do not repay evil with evil or insult with insult, but with blessing, because to this you were called so that you may inherit a blessing" (1 Pet. 3:9). Consider that last phrase: "called so that you may inherit a blessing." It is indeed a paradox that I can block my own inheritance by resisting praying blessings on those who insult me. Now, it was bad enough being insulted, but to miss a blessing because I am unwilling to bless in return is a double insult and I cause it myself.

When I use the forgiveness tool and bless someone who has insulted me, I can avoid being baited into entrapment— committing the same sin of worthless words: "The one determining to love life, and to see inherently good days, let him stop his tongue from worthlessness, and his lips not to speak baited entrapment. Let him turn away from worthlessness, and do inherent good; let him seek peace, and pursue it" (1 Pet. 3:10–11).[2]

To see good days, we need to develop the skill of repaying

evil with blessing. The reality of blocked blessings is truer than most ever realize. Don't block your blessings—use the tool of praying blessings on those challenging people and prepare for your inheritance. You can be on God's praise team daily through your prayers of blessings that you call down on those who offend you. You can move from being the victim of insult to being the captain of a praise team. As the psalmist prayed, "Don't leave the victims to rot in the street; make them a choir that sings your praises" (Ps. 74:20 THE MESSAGE).

Overcoming Evil with Good in the Twenty-first Century

Our heavenly Father is ready to help whenever we are being outwitted by the father of lies (see John 8:44). The outwitting ends when we confront the lies with truth. For longer than I would like to admit, Satan outwitted me in the area of unforgiveness. I assumed that I had really forgiven a particular person until someone's question exposed the unforgiveness that was still free-floating in my heart.

One day I was race-walking with a young pastor's wife, and she said, "May I ask you a personal question?" Then she asked me why I didn't like a particular person. I sensed that she was on to me but asked, "What do you mean?" She replied, "You are such a demonstrative person, Jackie. You are always full of compliments, but whenever this woman's name is mentioned, you become deadly silent." There's an expression for what happened to me in that moment: I was *busted!* The fact is I was harboring hurt feelings and anger toward the person. Although silence was better than slander, my silence was actually broadcasting my bad attitude.

That day was a turning point in understanding that unforgiveness in my heart is on display whether I am cognizant of it or not. How is this possible? Body language. Silence. Eighty percent of communication takes place without words. Subsequent to this young woman's question, I became deeply concerned about the other people in my life I hadn't forgiven and their awareness of it. I realized that my resentment was displayed on my body and through my silence like one of those big sandwich signs. That evening I asked my husband if he thought a particular family member was aware of the unforgiveness I held in my heart toward him and his wife. Without skipping a beat, Ken replied, "Absolutely! Jackie, you are normally so outgoing and friendly, but when you're responding to them, you are very reserved."

Before I went to sleep that night, I picked up the forgiveness tool. I prayed a blessing on this couple, and just as I finished my prayer, I felt something dislodge in my heart—it was a big ol' chunk of bitterness removed by this forgiving blessing. The next time I saw them, the love of God was flowing so freely through me toward them that I couldn't wait to give them both big bear hugs. Through that prayer of blessing over them, in that moment, I outwitted my excuse that they had never said, "I am sorry."

Don't Let Your Body Language or Your Silence Tell on You

Your body language and what you say or don't say are sure displays of your heart's condition—negative or positive. Warning: people know exactly how you feel about them, even when you haven't said a word. Your body—or your silence—is tattling on your heart. Research in the new field of social neuroscience is providing fresh insight into this process: "Our brains are designed to reflect and catch *the state of the person* we're with, which works to our advantage in most situations by helping us understand each other better," says Daniel Goleman, PhD, author of *Social Intelligence*.[3]

Smiles and flattery do not cover up unforgiveness marinating in your heart. Even when you choose silence, your heart's condition is being detected by those you are with. Remember what Paul told the Colossians:

> Make allowance for each other's faults, and forgive anyone who offends you. Remember, the Lord forgave you, so you must forgive others. Above all, clothe yourself with love, which binds us all together in perfect harmony. (Col. 3:13–14 NLT)

Offense is inevitable among humans. Therefore, we should wear the clothing of love so that making allowances will be spontaneous. *When it comes to offense, the original incident is the fault of the offender, but my allowing the incident to keep offending me is my choice.* I can forgive again and call down a blessing or respond in self-harm and be offended again. "Every time the grievance comes to mind, in fact, the body can re-create the emotional and physical duress that accompanied the original hurt. You become agitated; blood pressure soars; stress hormones are released. Forgiveness, however, can restore peacefulness and balance."[4]

Hopefully by this point you no longer want to simply forget about an injury—which is not always possible—but rather choose to move on by forgiving and by praying blessings on the offender. If you feel daunted by this challenge, read what Kristin Armstrong wrote:

The very idea of generating feelings of kindness for someone who has broken your heart seems at the very least ridiculous, and at the most...impossible. The trick is that it is not all about feelings. [Paul] doesn't say, "Feel kind and compassionate toward one another." He said, "Be kind and compassionate to one another." It's an order, requiring simple obedience, not emotion. Obedience springs from the love and desire to please God, nothing else.[5]

Praying Blessings Without Ceasing

Sometimes we have been blessed with very unlovable people in our lives. Sometimes their very *presence* is irritating. These unlovable people are given to us for our training to learn this wise principle: "A man's wisdom gives him patience; it is to his glory to overlook an offense" (Prov. 19:11).

Even selfless Mother Teresa had to learn this:

> There is one sister in the community who has the knack of rubbing me the wrong way at every turn; her mannerisms, her ways of speaking, her character strike me as unlovable. But then she's a sister; God must love her dearly; so I am not going to let my natural dislike of her get the best of me.
>
> Thus, I remind myself that Christian love is not a matter of feelings; it means doing things. I have determined to treat this sister as if she is the person I love best in the world. Every time I meet her, I pray for her, and I offer thanks to God for her virtues and her efforts. I feel certain that Jesus would like me to do this.[6]

Mother Teresa knew that praying blessings for this unlovable sister released her to be a display of God's forgiving love. When was the last time you prayed a blessing over someone who annoys you at work? When was the last time you prayed a blessing over someone in your family who annoys you regularly? Do you need to pause right now and pray a blessing over someone? Moving past an offense is a skill you can develop as you learn to resist the excuses of unforgiveness and utilize the forgiveness tool of praying blessings. These actions will help expedite your experience of glory.

We've looked at Hebrews 12:15: "Look after each other so that none of you fails to receive the grace of God. Watch out that no poisonous root of bitterness grows up to trouble you, corrupting many" (NLT). In another translation an interesting expression caught my attention: "Overseeing yourselves lest anyone fall short, being apart from the grace of God, lest any root of bitterness sprouting up mob you, and through it many be defiled."[7] The phrase "mob you" brings to mind all the celebrities who are constantly mobbed by their adoring fans and are afraid of being trampled. The unforgiveness in our hearts is like a mob of screaming fans—ready to trample our hearts beyond repair. Not being able to forgive someone else or even yourself puts you in a precarious place! There is great potential for being mobbed by bitterness that not only tramples the unforgiving one; it tramples all over those who are with that person. To prevent being mobbed and trampled by a root of bitterness, a very practical tool of forgiveness is available for you and me—when we pray blessings.

One of the greatest Christians was a glorious example of the application of the forgiveness tool of praying blessings. He lived it and wrote to other Christians, reminding them to do it even in the presence of the harshest treatment! "We bless those who curse us. We are patient with those who abuse us. We appeal gently when evil things are said about us. Yet we are treated like the world's garbage" (1 Cor. 4:12–13 NLT).

How could Paul bless those who cursed him? Not in his flesh but through his strong faith could he do what Jesus asked of him. Too many believers want God's blessing, but they don't want to bless those who are difficult, ruthless, or miserable—which all of us are at times.

Some Get to Hear, "I Am Sorry"

When we forgive, we place ourselves in position to witness a wonderful miracle. I gave the gift of forgiveness to my mother-in-law for years of rejection. I did this long before she asked my forgiveness. For years I displayed love toward her, all the while knowing she was not pleased with me. But by the power of Christ, I kept living forgiveness, which means living love, and I did this without any promise of reciprocation.

After two decades of doing what was right, forgiving again and again, I discovered the Lord had an amazing plan. It occurred when my mother-in-law was very ill and needed help around the house. The wonderful woman who came to help her and Papa was a great caregiver but not a good cook. After hearing so many complaints about the food, I suggested to my sister-in-law that we start taking meals to Mimi (Esther) and Papa. Trust me, such an act of service could only flow from a forgiving heart informed by the Holy Spirit. After several weeks of my cooking for them, one of my nieces went by to have lunch with them, and when she complimented the food, Mimi said, "Your aunt Jackie made it." Following that one simple remark, my niece asked Mimi if they could speak alone after lunch.

With tears in her eyes, my niece began to talk to Mimi about what she had observed for years: Mimi's lack of unconditional love for her aunt Jackie. Mimi began to cry and told her granddaughter that she had wanted to ask my forgiveness for the longest time but was fearful. My niece encouraged her to act as promptly as possible.

If you can imagine the magnitude of this, my mother-in-law called to ask my forgiveness. I know that might be the most incomprehensible thing some of you have read in these pages, but that's why we know it was the Lord! The first thing I said to her was, "Mimi, have you felt loved by me all these years?" And her reply was, "Yes, you have always been so good to me." Then I said, "Mimi, that proves I forgave you a long time ago, and I have continued to live forgiveness by loving you even when I knew you struggled with loving me." She cried so hard. She actually called me two days later to make sure I had really forgiven her.

I then called my sister-in-law to tell her about this amazing event, and she shared an extraordinary fact with me that knocked my socks off. She told me that she and my nieces had been praying "behind my back" that Mimi would ask my forgiveness for the way she had treated me. They prayed this prayer for several years. They were prayer warriors on my behalf!

Before Mimi went to be with Jesus, we had a Thanksgiving gathering and she spoke to all of us about what she was grateful for, and the last thing she said was a glowing tribute to the fruitfulness of my life. Everyone was crying, but when Mimi blessed me with kind words, my nieces and children and husband all looked at me, beaming with joy and knowing that Mimi was ready to see the One who allows us to forgive freely—even if it is during the last days of our journeys on this planet.

Note: The forgiveness tool of praying a blessing is not a magic incantation. It is a fortifying tool for the one who desires to forgive effectively. This is not a tool with which we can manipulate God or other people; rather, using it aligns our hearts with the heart of the Great Forgiver. This tool allows you to strengthen your identity as one who forgives—and free yourself to love. In the next chapter, we will learn about another tool that is a great preparation for resisting future situations of captivity to unforgiveness.

MAKE IT PERSONAL

1. Before reading this chapter, had you decided that you couldn't forgive until you heard "I am sorry"? Have you changed your mind?

2. "[Jesus] was aware that forgiving his enemies was a proactive defense against any temptation to become embittered toward them....We're watching a Savior who is protecting Himself against the temptation of hatred and resentment." Do you think that's why Jesus forgave the Roman soldiers? Why or why not? (See Luke 23:34.)

3. Read Job 42:7–10. Have you ever prayed blessings on your offender(s)? If so, what happened? (See 1 Pet. 3:9.)

4. Are you offended by the suggestion of praying a blessing on your offender? (See Rom. 5:8; Col. 3:13–14.)

5. "What was done *to* us will be healed by what was done *for* us." What does this statement mean to you?

6. Read Job 42:10 and describe the embedded blessing within the forgiveness tool of praying blessings on one's offender(s). Is this a new concept for you? Have you ever seen it happen?

7. Examine Proverbs 25:21–22 and list the blessings we can hinder when we don't forgive (see Prov. 19:11).

8. Were you surprised by the fact that your body and your silence are sure displays of your heart's condition of unforgiveness? Have you ever noticed resentment in someone else's countenance?

Chapter 10

Forgiveness Tool of Exposing Unrealistic Expectations

I used to assume that a person's propensity to being easily offended flowed only from a wounded heart. But the more I have considered the impact of expectations, the more I see something else that feeds one's vulnerability to offense. Our high, often unrealistic expectations of life, family, love, career, and purpose can all be subtle preparation for offense. Expectations actually exacerbate our vulnerability to offense.

If you are willing to evaluate your expectations of the people in your life, God will transform your resistance to forgive. This forgiveness tool can change you from being a person who is vulnerable to offense into a person strengthened in his or her identity of one who forgives.

Probably the most widespread defense against forgiving is someone's repeated offense, as we discussed in detail in chapter 6. People feel justified in their unforgiving condition because of the understandable frustration that comes from being offended again and again. Nevertheless, by now I am presuming you understand that in the context of the cross of Jesus, there are no excuses for the Christian to not forgive. The truth of God's Word reminds you and me to forgive...and forgive again, aggressively resisting any excuse not to forgive, regardless of whether the offense is marginal or unimaginable. So how does one work through the aggravation of having to forgive again?

First of all, we need to honestly evaluate how irritated we actually get when having to forgive someone again. Answer the hard questions: Why are we so annoyed with repeated offense? What is the energy and stimuli behind our exasperation at having to forgive someone again? Could our emotional response to another offense possibly reveal the time spent rereading our infamous grudge books? Perhaps we have been looking through the decorative, laminated ledgers enumerating all the offenses committed by another person, studying those debit columns with all the entries of dates, times, and what was done. The credit column is sadly empty—no room for a grace entry.

People Are Just People

Scripture tells us, "People are born for trouble as readily as sparks fly up from a fire" (Job 5:7 NLT). Our level of frustration with people's offenses is directly proportionate to our expectations of their behavior. Indeed, my own expectations set the very framework for my being offended again. And, while life provides predictable trouble, God provides equally predictable vouchers of grace (see James 4:6). Sometimes we resist God's grace and stay in our anger. Rather than sip God's refreshing grace, we guzzle down a glass of toxic bitterness.

"Surely resentment destroys the fool, and jealousy kills the simple" (Job 5:2 NLT).

One day my son shared a quote with me that describes this condition precisely. The quote so captured my heart that I wrote it on a slip of paper and taped it to the dashboard of my car: "Expectations are premeditated resentment."[1]

Throughout that day, as I drove around doing errands, I replayed hundreds of situations from my life where I could clearly trace the expectations that preceded the resentment in my heart. Anne Lamott says unforgiveness is like drinking poison and hoping the rat dies. If my expectations are inextricably linked to premeditated resentment, then I am poisoning myself when I don't immediately commit those expectations to God (see Ps. 62:5). Just as we are encouraged in the Word to take our thoughts captive (see 2 Cor. 10:5), I envision carrying a leather lasso so I can take captive any expectation that comes into my heart and tie that expectation to the cross.

As the Lord brought to my mind the trickling-down resentment in my heart, I thought of Ephesians 4:31: "Get rid of all bitterness, rage and anger." Why? Because these grieve the Holy Spirit (see Eph. 4:30). "Bitterness" in this passage refers to something being "pressed down."[2] "Anger" in this verse refers to "desire, violent passion."[3] Aristotle called this kind of anger "desire plus grief." When my violent desires are not met, when my expectations are not fulfilled, the grief that follows is ultimately converted into resentment.

With all my premeditated resentments, it is no wonder I am prone to offense. I heard Brennan Manning say at a conference, "Expectations are our subtle attempt to control God and manipulate mystery." I must begin with God, asking His forgiveness for my controlling expectations. Then I ask His forgiveness for all the slow-burning resentment in my heart because of so much desire mixed with grief. So many expectations of myself...of others...of life. So much unnecessary stuff to "press down" in bitterness.

Besides seeking God's forgiveness, I need to seek His guidance. Only by availing myself of *His* expectations of my life can I relinquish my own. The Holy Spirit reminds us to give our blueprints and dreams to the Lord for His authorization on a continual basis. He tells us to preface our plans with the expression "If the Lord wills":

> You who say, "Today or tomorrow we are going to a certain town and will stay there a year. We will do business there and make a profit."...What you ought to say is, "If the Lord wants us to, we will live and do this or that." Otherwise you are boasting about your own plans, and all such boasting is evil. (James 4:13, 15–16 NLT)

I am still a planner, dreamer, and list maker, but I am using the phrase "If the Lord wills..." more than ever these days.

I Want a "Ten," but I Keep Getting a "Five"

A woman I know went to a professional counselor about her battle with depression. If you looked at this woman's life, you would wonder how she could be depressed. But having it all has not kept her from constantly struggling with a low-grade fever that runs through her soul. Recently, she had an epiphany in the counselor's office when she was introduced to the principle of wanting a "ten life in a five world." The counselor helped her see that she wants a life that rates a perfect score of ten, but life outside the Garden of Eden too often rates a five. This woman's absurd expectations were fueling her constant trouble with depression.

In various ways, we all are like this woman. We want to be able to attend family gatherings or go to work without ever being offended. Hey, we just want to be able to sit at our kitchen tables and not risk getting offended! But when a person expects perfection, she is going to have a day that will be more of a five than a ten. If you prepare to go to an event, especially one where you were previously offended, accept its potential as a five. If it turns out to be an eight, you'll leave feeling as if you've received a bonus!

Holidays and Premeditated Resentment

I love holidays, and I make the time to prepare the many things that make a holiday most memorable with loved ones. Yet one thing I tend to forget in my preparations for a specific celebration is to prepare my heart for the reality of potential disappointment and offense. Too often I am outwitted by the same relative who repeats offensive behavior during such a festive celebration. I can have my house decorated just as I imagined and the food all turns out perfectly, but then I forget to remind my heart that life is always more chaotic than predictable. I need to leave room for this much-anticipated event not to be the ten I dreamed of but a five. I also need to be realistic that even on a most precious holiday like Christmas, I may need to forgive someone I love for doing something that offends me.

Was last Christmas a disaster because of a selfish relative? Perhaps the previous Thanksgiving was pretty pathetic because of the unresolved conflict that put a real chill in the air—even if you live in hot south Florida. Holiday preparations need to include the emotional care of one's own heart in anticipation of the inevitable need to forgive again and pray blessings. Keep in mind, if there are human beings attending a holiday event, offense may happen—even if the clash occurs when sulking silence meets brooding melancholy.

The following two letters I received indicate that these people understand what it is to moderate expectations:

> I think it is so hard to forgive those in authority particularly: pastors, parents, even spouse because we have a misconception and belief that they are here to support us. They are supposed to meet our needs when in fact they are NOT, but God IS.
>
> And He alone can!
>
> Our parents have a duty to provide, yes, but we cannot expect them to meet our every need. Only God can do that.
>
> Our church leadership/pastors are here to help and support us, help us, yes. They love and have compassion, but churches and pastors are instituted by God for the purpose of ministering to and guiding us toward a closer walk with God, directing us back to the One who does meet all of our needs.
>
> In marriage, when we have set up wrong expectations (either way, husband or wife), we place an unnecessary strain on the person, creating an idol in our hearts and the relationship suffers.
>
> I think this is what keeps us from forgiving, not looking enough to our own sin and how we might have believed a lie from the enemy and acted out of that in not forgiving.
>
> When any relationship becomes out of whack with what it was designed for, we hurt one another and become unforgiving!

Our focus needs to be shifted to Jesus, the One and Only! And [we need to] keep a loose touch on our fellow co-laborers.

When we look at Jesus' nail-scarred hands, how can we hold anything against anyone else? We have been given and forgiven so much!

—*Katarina Juliao*

I once held great anger and unforgiveness toward certain family members. I believed that they had the choice, as I did, to act in a loving way, and if that was not possible to get professional help. They chose not to get help and held me responsible for a failed relationship. However, even though I chose not to put myself in the path of their destructiveness, I came to the place of forgiveness when I understood where they came from, and what parts of their backgrounds led them to their choices. This is what I describe as honoring my family: understanding where they came from and, while not agreeing with their choices, accepting their actions as choices made, and mine as strength to gain from the experience.

Still, there are other people in my life I find it hard to forgive.

What keeps me from forgiving? As I was rewriting this paragraph...I understood: I am unforgiving when the most vulnerable parts of me have been exposed, when promises of unconditional love are not kept...and it's my own fault—because I have sought to be protected (not rejected) and loved (not ostracized) by someone other than God...and then gotten angry when someone has failed me (as if their world revolved around me, and as if they could even come close to being God). Wow. Call that a therapeutic writing....

—*Chris Miller (teacher/artist)*

Manna and My Expectations

When you recognize that you are vulnerable to offense and need to pick up the forgiveness tool of evaluating unrealistic expectations, you are going to need sustenance for your work—heavenly sustenance. God provides this for you, in fact this "bread from heaven," this "food of angels" (Ps. 78:24–25 NLT), will nourish your soul whenever you encounter a repeated offense. Look at Deuteronomy 8:3:

> He humbled you, allowed you to hunger, and fed you with manna which you did not know nor did your fathers know, that He might make you know that man shall not live by bread alone; but man lives by every word that proceeds from the mouth of the LORD. (NKJV)

Understanding the meaning of "manna" can help you when others offend again. Manna is defined as "What?" or "What is this?"[4] When I am hit with back-to-back offenses, when there is a sudden shift in all that I expected from someone I love, I am quick to think, *What is this?* The answer is that *this* is the allotment of my daily manna.

God is teaching me that my response is to recognize that *this very circumstance* is my manna. *My manna is meant to provoke spiritual hunger.* One of the key phrases in Deuteronomy 8:3 is "allowed you to hunger." Manna is the daily provision of what my soul needs so that I will hunger for the Word of God.

Lately, so many things have gone wrong, and I've started saying to myself, "It's just my manna allotment today!" When the chaos escalates, I am calmed in my spirit when I remember I am just gathering manna. Maybe your manna today is to forgive a spouse or a child who is not living up to your expectations.

Sometimes the manna given us seems particularly unappetizing, and we may want to stay in our tents and not go out and pick it up. However, in the same way that manna would rot if kept until the next day (see Exod. 16:19–20), trying to avoid the reality of what is hard in our lives will only cause rottenness to develop in our souls.

Take heart! Whatever is happening in your life today is just your manna—spiritual-hunger-producing circumstances. Look at what I found in Revelation 2:17: "He who has an ear, let him hear what the Spirit says to the churches. To him who overcomes, I will give some of the hidden manna." A reward for overcoming life's trials and temptations is heavenly manna. When I am clinging to Jesus in a dark, trying hour, I can count on the necessary manna. And when I arrive victorious on heaven's shore, I will already have a prepared palate for heaven's manna.

The Word is my manna, my spiritual food today, and the Word will sustain me throughout eternity. While I've never developed an appetite for sushi, I sure have a ferocious appetite for manna. So, when you face your next trial, just whisper "manna," and realize that your palate is being trained for angels' food.

One Person Can Ruin Your Day— Because of Your Expectations

A man named Haman in the book of Esther was filled with rage toward a Jewish man named Mordecai. What Haman expected from Mordecai—to bow in honor—he never received, because being a devout Jew, Mordecai bowed only to the God of heaven. Haman was so offended by the way this one man treated him that he declared he could not enjoy the blessings of his own life.

> Haman went out that day happy and in high spirits. But when he saw Mordecai at the king's gate and observed that he neither rose nor showed fear in his presence, he was filled with rage against Mordecai. Nevertheless, Haman restrained himself and went home. Calling together his friends and Zeresh, his wife, Haman boasted to them about his vast wealth, his many sons, and all the ways the king had honored him and how he had elevated him above the other nobles and officials. "And that's not all," Haman added. "I'm the only person Queen Esther invited to accompany the king to the banquet she gave. And she has invited me along with the king tomorrow. *But all this gives me no satisfaction as long as I see that Jew Mordecai sitting at the king's gate.*" (Est. 5:9–13, emphasis added)

In a split second Haman went from happiness to rage, from good spirits to the darkest thoughts. Haman's expectation of Mordecai was the speedy transport train to offense that Haman rode that day, and Mordecai's lack of respect and honor was his ticket aboard.

What captivated me when I studied this passage was yet another example that people can be completely blinded to all their blessings by their internal rage toward an offensive person. What is robbing you of your joy in the blessings God has given you? What person holds you hostage to internal rage, potentially deadening any satisfaction with your life?

Until I learned these forgiveness principles, I, too, often was like Haman, robbed of the satisfaction of God's many blessings as I focused on the offenders in my life. In the book of Esther, Haman ends up at the end of a noose. Unforgiveness is ultimately the suffocation and strangling of my soul.

> Unrealistic or exaggerated expectations inevitably will cause others to fall short and offend us. Some desire their spouse or pastor or friends to meet their every need. However, at the deepest level, our soul was created to find its security in God, not man....The very power of our expectations can choke out the sweetness of a personal relationship. Suppose that, instead of burdening people with our expectations, we simply learned to appreciate them for themselves—no strings attached. What if we approach family and friends with gratitude for what they are doing rather than disappointment for what they failed to do? Suppose that a husband, instead of expecting a full-course dinner from his wife each night, learned to appreciate whatever she was able to offer him? Then, instead of his failed expectation degrading into an offense, there would be a living, sincere appreciation for the food his wife prepared. I know we have arrangements by common consent, but in reality, a wife is under no obligation to cook special meals or do housekeeping. You did not marry her to be your housekeeper, but to become one with her.
>
> You see, expectations can seem like legitimate aspects of a relationship, but they can also cause us to be disappointed and offended when people fall short. I have known situations in the past where my expectations actually blinded me to the efforts being made by a loved one. They were trying to improve in an area I was unaware of because my focus was preset upon a different expectation.[5]

Deadly Me-Centric Living

People who live self-centered lives are prone to offense because they grow up thinking life should be on their terms. When I hear about the teen suicide rate increasing in our wealthy nation, I can't help but wonder about the "noose of expectations."

Have we carelessly neglected the dangerous strangulation of life through an attitude of entitlement? One can almost understand a person taking his life if he is living a horror story, but when two teenage brothers who live in the wealthiest part of Atlanta take their lives, we must ask ourselves what was so incapacitating that suicide was the only alternative. Have we crippled our children by allowing them to be so "me-centric" that they are unable to handle the reality of life on this painful planet—life that is not always going to be about them? Have we so exaggerated our children's value that they expect, like Haman, to be treated like royalty and are absolutely incapacitated when they don't get the treatment they expect?

Me-centric living does not allow a child or an adult ever to move into the Olympic gold circle of being most like Jesus through learning to forgive freely. Forgiveness is so other-centered and so God-centered that the me-centric person is unlikely to have the faith or even the desire to forgive another for not catering to his or her demanding spirit.

Each person on this planet is marked by the fingerprints of the Creator—but this does not entitle us to receive worship. Me-centric expectations flow from someone who has been worshiped. Me-centric people can indeed be transformed by Jesus to focus on others rather than solely on themselves; but when they finally see this truth, they will have to forgive those (parents/mates) who worshiped them and cost them a realistic view of life outside the Garden of Eden.

Reality Check for All People Living Outside the Garden

One day a mother walks her child to the school bus pickup area. She watches her child get on the bus, but no sooner does he step on than he turns around and gets off. The child then walks over to the mother and announces, "I am not going to school. It is too hard and too boring." The mother's loving reply to her child's remark: "Welcome to the real world, honey. Now get back on the bus." You may find that mother's response harsh, but I had to learn much later in life that life is unfair, hard, and often boring.

God's way to heaven, this wonderful gift package, includes not only heaven but also a more abundant life on this planet. At this stage of my life, I totally believe John 10:10 in its declaration that Jesus came to give us life more abundantly. I simply had to learn the hard way that "more abundantly" did not mean a life that was always fair, always easy, and never boring.

Learning this hard but needed truth changed my attitude as a mom. I did not want my children to grow up and struggle with the disillusionment that I had fought throughout my twenties and early thirties. As early as I can remember, I started teaching my children (when appropriate) that life is not always fair. Many times I have seen people angry at God because they confused life with God. Many adults were raised by parents who allowed their children to be more comfortable with illusion and fairy tales than with the realities of life's unfairness.

I am not a cynic. I love being alive. And in fact, knowing that life will sometimes be very unfair does not cause me sadness; it prepares me for the battle to trust God in the midst of unfairness. Therefore, when tragedy or disappointment knocks on the front door of our house, we do not need to run for the Emerald City. Instead, we grab Jesus' hand and together we open the door and allow disappointment and unfairness a place in the whole context of the Kendall family.

The wisest king of Israel understood clearly that life is often unfair, yet God can be a greater reality:

> I have seen something else under the sun:
>> The race is not to the swift
>>> or the battle to the strong,
>> nor does food come to the wise
>>> or wealth to the brilliant
>>> or favor to the learned;
>> but time and chance happen to them all. (Eccl. 9:11)

To effectively rein in unrealistic expectations, we need to soberly consider the length of our lives here on the planet. The more I am aware of the limited day-pass I have—that my life is a passing shadow—the less I am willing to waste unholy sweat clinging to what I *expect* rather than embracing what is the *reality* of my life. Living on Planet Earth with six billion sinners (I among them) guarantees the daily inevitability of offense. I need to be armed with the tools of forgiveness so that resentment, bitterness, and anger do not use up my limited day-pass.

Recently my son, Ben, and I were discussing the age-old question that has been front and center for philosophers for centuries: "Why do bad things happen to good people?" Ben was so excited, because he had just heard someone say, "From a biblical perspective, that question is flawed. There are actually no good people." Consider Jesus' response to a ruler who called him "good": "A certain ruler asked him, 'Good teacher, what must I do to inherit eternal life?' 'Why do you call me good?' Jesus answered. 'No one is good—except God alone'" (Luke 18:18–19).

Jesus was not being overly humble; He was making a critical point. Even on my best day, I am still flawed and not innately good. If I do good things, it is a manifestation of a soul kissed by grace. The psalmist reflected, "Seventy years are given to us! Some even live to eighty. But even the best years are filled with pain and trouble; soon they disappear, and we fly away" (Ps. 90:10 NLT).

The struggle to forgive is part of the pain and trouble we face in our seventy or more years on this earth. The issue of needing to forgive someone will no longer exist only when we no longer exist.

We have unrealistic expectations when we are surprised that we have to forgive a loved one again. How often have you been shocked that a loved one spoke something hurtful? More than once? During the early years of my marriage, my heart was so wounded that my mouth was often an instrument of harm. Sarcasm and cruel criticism were a common experience for those around me. When my husband began to express how hurtful my remarks were, I sought professional help for rage that seemed to flow from my heart. While I was getting help with my heart wounds, I would often fail and say something hurtful again. When I asked Ken's forgiveness, he would often reply, in stark honesty, "It is hard for me to forgive you, Jackie, because I know you will probably do it again."

Ken reasoned that true sorrow would keep me from ever offending in that way again. "If you were really sorry," he would often say, "you would never speak such toxic phrases." By the grace of God, we have come a long way from those days, and my husband is not nearly as hesitant to forgive when I ask. He now knows that he is living with a flawed yet faithful child of God, which requires him to be a great forgiver. I, myself, often had to forgive Ken for not being willing to forgive me as freely as I forgave his judgmental attitude. Be careful about putting conditions on your forgiveness, or your inner peace will depend on the decision of the person who hurt you.

> "Watch yourselves. If your brother sins, rebuke him, and if he repents, forgive him. If he sins against you seven times in a day, and seven times comes back to you and says, 'I repent,' forgive him."
> The apostles said to the Lord, "Increase our faith!" (Luke 17:3–5)

Notice that the apostles' response to forgiving a brother seven times in one day would require an "increase" in faith. As my husband's faith grew, his ability to forgive me seven times in one day became a developed skill. Has Jesus ever forgiven you for the same offense?

Remember, we need forgiveness as much as we need to forgive:

> *Forgiveness is sometimes so infuriating! I have been so badly hurt, and now, just because they ask me to forgive them, or because God instructs me to forgive them, they get off scot-free. That just doesn't seem fair. I want justice, and the ease with which the other person can walk away free and clear because I*

let them go oftentimes feels too easy. It should be more difficult for them to get out of their crime. They should have to get stretched on the rack a little bit, or give at least a little bit of blood. That is what I want to do to them anyway. I can remember one decisive moment this past summer when I knew the only way out of a conflict with my bride was to forgive her. I knew I had the choice either to hold my anger or let it go and let her go free. It just seemed too easy. I wanted her to pay for wounding me. But I let her go free (that time) and just marveled at the grace the Lord bestowed on me when He let me go free for all my wounds to Him. It also was eye-opening, since I recognized through it how many times she lets me go free without me even realizing I had wounded her.

—Andrew Holbrook

Resist Resentment Toward God Because of Unrealistic Expectations

The conditions I place on forgiveness too often parallel my unrealistic expectations. Too many Christians have expected presumptuously that they would be protected from suffering because of the abundant life promised by Jesus in John chapter 10. I have met some young believers who actually think that their growing relationship with Jesus is immunization against suffering. Of course, anyone who is sober (not anesthetizing his or her pain) has been exposed to suffering and disappointment. All suffering provides a choice for the individual: trust God, or angrily doubt His goodness. As Oswald Chambers wrote, "Extraordinary things happen for the person who hangs on to God's love, when the odds are against God's character."[6]

When you and I cling to the facts about the goodness of God, even when we have experienced the seemingly unforgivable, such tenacity of faith produces a perspective of finally seeing God's fingerprints all over our past and present. If, on the other hand, you and I refuse to believe that God is good and resist clinging to our hope in Him, we forfeit seeing His fingerprints on our lives. It is in resisting God's love and clinging to my bitterness like a favorite blanket that bitterness thrives.

Remember what Paul wrote:

> Our present troubles are small and won't last very long. Yet they produce for us a glory that vastly outweighs them and will last forever! (2 Cor. 4:17 NLT)

> Momentary, light affliction is producing for us an eternal weight of glory far beyond all comparison. (2 Cor. 4:17 NASB)

If suffering lasted forever, one could not even consider trusting in God's love and goodness. But whatever we suffer is only momentary in comparison to the glory that will be ours for trusting Him in suffering. Suffering is a great instructor for those who have growing faith. Recently I found this nugget in Paul's second letter to the Corinthians:

> Rather, as servants of God we commend ourselves in every way: in great endurance; in troubles, hardships and distresses; in beatings...in purity, understanding, patience and kindness; in the Holy Spirit and in sincere love; in truthful speech and in the power of God; *with*

weapons of righteousness in the right hand and in the left. (2
Cor. 6:4–7, emphasis added)

One of the many benefits of hardships and battles is that we
become trained warriors or gladiators who go into battle with
weapons in both hands! God used that passage to cast a discerning light on the hardships of the last year—the benefits of
training me to carry weapons of righteousness in both hands!
In Psalm 18:34, David referred to God training his hands for
battle, and the word translated "training" in Hebrew means "to
be accustomed to."[7] I know that one of the benefits of battle
is the hope of living through it; and by training, being accustomed to battle, we will not be thrown seemingly unforgivable offenses. Forgiveness requires much trust, and the pain of
being offended can be used for either good or evil. A Japanese
poet by the name of Kenji Miyazawa captured the redeeming
aspect of one's suffering: "We must embrace pain and burn it
as fuel for our journey."[8]

Too many people allow the unforgiveness in their hearts to
produce the crude fuel of anger and bitterness. Good forgivers
learn to develop a purer fuel for their life journeys: grace, flowing from a heart of trust in the Great Forgiver.

Does Trying to Forgive Sting Like a Scorpion?

Ezekiel not only had to give up the dream of serving in the temple
in Jerusalem, he was forewarned about his audience, his congregation, his flock: "Son of man, do not fear them or their words.
Don't be afraid even though their threats surround you like net-
tles and briers and stinging scorpions. Do not be dismayed by
their dark scowls, even though they are rebels" (Ezek. 2:6 NLT).

What would be my response to such an assignment? *Forget it! I am going to quit this job and go and be a greeter at Wal-Mart!* How many times have you been stung by a scorpion when you have attempted to share your hope in Jesus? How many times has the Lord brought a wounded person into your life whom you tried to help, but in the process you were stung?

I am convinced that when we are stung, God's grace is the antiseptic and His glory is the Band-Aid. Yes, we will get stung in life and in ministry, but be of good cheer—we will not die from the sting. More often we are harmed by our anger over being stung (see Gal. 6:9)!

One other aspect of painful forgiving is that we fail to recognize the offender's blindness. When a person is blind emotionally and spiritually, his or her offensive behavior will sometimes catch you off guard. The wiser you become, the more you will expect brazen audacity from blind people. My father never admitted that he sexually abused some of his children, and he responded furiously when confronted about it. It takes great maturity to forgive not only the offender but also his brazen audacity! God says, "Call on me when you are in trouble, and I will rescue you, and you will give me glory" (Ps. 50:15 NLT).

Only an Eagle Can Handle Repeated Offenses

A dear friend of mine used to raise turkeys on her parents' farm. She told me that if you don't help a turkey get into the barn when a storm is coming, it will stand squawking with fear, and with beak wide open, will drown in a storm. By contrast, when an eagle senses that a storm is approaching, it will spread its wings and begin to ride the air currents. The eagle soars with the anticipation of climbing higher and higher on these strong winds—enjoying a great time of soaring.

If we respond to offense like turkeys, we can drown; if we respond like eagles, we can rise and soar. I have seen people flee like squawking turkeys, running under the barn when it comes to the challenge of forgiving someone who has offended them. Have you found yourself nearly drowning in a storm of offense?

It's natural for me to act like a turkey, standing and yelling about experiencing another offense. But I have chosen by faith to be an eagle in my spirit. I spread my wings of faith to embrace the strong winds and soar into this new storm of offense and anticipate the miracles and insight that are available only on a higher level of soaring and forgiving!

> He gives strength to the weary
>   and increases the power of the weak.
> Even youths grow tired and weary,
>   and young men stumble and fall;
> but those who hope in the LORD [spread their wings by faith]
>   will renew their strength.
> They will soar on wings like eagles;
>   they will run and not grow weary,
>   they will walk and not be faint. (Isa. 40:29–31)

Unforgiveness is like a bird in a cage. The bird is constrained—kept from doing the very thing the bird was created to do. With the cage door closed, the bird is sitting on its perch—with wings that are not free to soar. Can you imagine an eagle in a birdcage? As ridiculous as that visual is, so is the Christian living with unforgiveness in his heart. Unforgiveness keeps one locked in a cage—not using one's wings to soar, but only dreaming about being free to soar and love.

MAKE IT PERSONAL

1. When have you connected resentment to an unmet expectation? (See Job 5:2 NLT.)

2. Consider how many offenses you have experienced this year that arose from your expectations of a loved one. How can you begin to change this habit? (See Ps. 62:5.)

3. Do you tend to expect a ten world? Are you shocked when it's usually a five? Share an example. How can you begin to modify your expectations? (See Ps. 16:5; Eccl. 9:11.)

4. Have you ever conceived of heavenly manna as a reward for overcoming trials? (See Deut. 8:3; Rev. 2:17.)

5. Can you think of one person you can count on to ruin your day? How does he or she do this? How can *you* change so you're not offended as often? (See Est. 5:9–13; 2 Cor. 4:17.)

6. Do you find yourself focused on "me-centric" living? What are three ways you can begin to change to other-centered living?

7. Are you angered when a loved one offends you *again*? Why is anger an unreasonable response for the Christian? (See Luke 17:3–5.)

8. Does asking you to forgive still feel like the sting of a scorpion? If so, why? (See Ezek. 2:6 NLT.)

9. Do you react to offense like a turkey or an eagle? (See Ps. 90:10 NLT; Isa. 40:29–31; Ps. 50:15.)

Chapter 11

Forgiveness Tool of Growing Faith

G iving your excuses to God to be transformed is not possible even with the strongest of character. This gesture requires a living and growing *faith*. Just as I have said from the beginning, forgiveness is inextricably linked to one's faith. Whether it is the acceptance of forgiveness or the giving of forgiveness, it is not accomplished without the component of a growing faith.

If you have been struggling with the suggestion to appropriate a forgiveness tool or even to let go of your excuses for unforgiveness, this struggle can be traced to the faith content of your heart. Growing faith provides the strength to present excuses to God for their transformation into liberating forgiveness tools. In turn, the strength to actually use the forgiveness tool comes from faith. In fact, as your faith develops, you can wield a forgiveness tool in each hand! By faith I can look at an incident with realistic expectations and then move into the prayer of blessings on the person who shattered another of my unrealistic dreams! These tools will help you resist future hostage situations—held hostage to unforgiveness.

M. E. Cravens, my first Christian counselor, gave me a verse that was life-impacting: "You will keep in perfect peace him whose mind is steadfast, because he trusts in you" (Isa. 26:3).

This verse presented a major challenge to me as a young woman with such deep heart wounds. The peace promised in this verse so often was beyond my reach because of the storm that raged in my heart through all the unforgiven offenses. In this verse, "steadfast" and "trusts" challenge me to live firmly attached to Jesus. In recent days, this verse has made me think of being sort of handcuffed to Jesus, who alone can provide friendly reassurance rather than condemning correction when I am afraid and fearful. God wants to guard and protect (keep)[1] my heart, but He can do this only if I have chosen firm attachment through the mental discipline of trusting rather than defaulting to anxiety and fear.

God wants to guard and protect us as a loving shepherd. "Like a shepherd, he will care for his flock, gathering the lambs in his arms, hugging them as he carries them, leading the nursing ewes to good pasture" (Isa. 40:11 THE MESSAGE). I love the image of a shepherd not only lifting his lambs up but also hugging them as he holds them. That image of God may not be comprehendable for you at this time, but I hope that you will come to know it intimately.

One of my favorite Scriptures is Deuteronomy 33:12: "Let the beloved of the LORD rest secure in him, for he shields him all day long, and the one the LORD loves rests between his shoulders." Recently I looked up the word translated "rest," and a new image came. It means "to reside, inhabit, dwell, abide."[2] There is a meaning of permanence in these words; to "rest" is much more than taking a pit stop during one of life's storms. Resting in our heavenly Shepherd's arms, on His lap, is where we set up house. The safest place on this earth is the lap of God. I see my favorite pillow and comforter on His lap and myself snuggling in and resting, even during another emotional hurricane in my life.

Heart wounds are not healed instantaneously. The patience of a resting lamb is imperative. A Hebrew name for God that gives this resting-lamb confidence is *Jehovah-mekkodishkim*. This name means "the God who sanctifies."[3] Sanctification is just a fancy name for daily becoming a little more like Jesus. Sanctification is a lifelong process. Heart-wound healing is instantaneous only for the detached person who lives on Denial Avenue. The length of time required for healing is in proportion to the depth of the offense. Some people have many offenses that they need to recover from. God is keenly aware of all we need to bravely forgive.

> You did it: you changed wild lament
>   into whirling dance;
> You ripped off my black mourning band
>   and decked me with wildflowers.
> I'm about to burst with song;
>   I can't keep quiet about you.
> GOD, my God,
>   I can't thank you enough. (Ps. 30:11–12 THE MESSAGE)

What Healing — and Facing Unforgiveness — Requires

How does one develop the confidence to be a lap-resting lamb? M. E. Cravens taught me something that has become the foundation of my ability to trust God, even with soul-deadening heart wounds. She challenged me to take a red pencil, read through all the Psalms, and circle the word *trust* whenever I read it in a verse. She knew that one of the key methods for healing my troubled heart would be through a consistent, daily time in God's Word. She gave me the "red circle of trust project" to begin the internal healing of my heart.

Professor Cravens knew the penetrating power of God's Word, since she herself had been healed of heinous heart wounds and was sharing the method with me. In one of our first sessions, she said to me, "Jackie, God wants to bring good out of this evil, but the confidence and trust in God's capacity to do so will require a consistent, daily growing relationship with God through His Word." I had already developed a daily time of reading God's Word, but now I realized it was not only a "holy sweat discipline," it was the very method for God to heal my broken heart.

Spending time daily in God's Word accustoms me to being drenched in His satisfaction with me! Too many people want to heal a deep heart wound with an "emergency room" relationship with God. They call on Him and want His participation in their lives only during trouble. However, an enormous heart wound will be healed only by a constant, deep relationship with God, a relationship that allows Him to touch the various aspects of daily life. Is He a part of the dailies of your life?

Time spent in God's Word is one of the ways God chips away at some of the hardness in my heart. We've got calluses on our hearts from years of swallowing hurts and disappointments and unforgiveness. God's Word begins the healing process: "The Word of God is alive and powerful. It is sharper than the sharpest two-edged sword, cutting between soul and spirit, between joint and marrow. It exposes our innermost thoughts and desires" (Heb. 4:12 NLT).

Do you realize that trust and time in God's Word are inextricably linked? Have you considered that your faith is empowered and enhanced through regular time spent reading God's Word? Or does reading the Bible still seem unrelated to the healing of your heart? It is too dangerous to consider looking into a painful past and dealing with the need to forgive the seemingly unforgivable without the fortification of a growing faith in Jesus. That faith is fostered in the Word.

Jerry Bridges wrote:

> God's unfailing love for us is an objective fact affirmed over and over in the Scriptures. It is true whether we believe it or not. Our doubts do not destroy God's love, nor does our faith create it.... But the experience of that love and the comfort it is intended to bring is dependent upon our believing the truth about God's love as it is revealed to us in Scriptures. Doubts about God's love, allowed to harbor in our hearts, will surely deprive us of the comfort of His love.[4]

I cannot appropriate God's comfort and love apart from confidence in His presence in my life. Bitter and cynical Christians develop when people's pain exceeds their faith. Has your faith been outrun by your pain? Doubting God's love deprives us of the comfort we desperately need. Our doubts prevent us from having access to the heavenly salve of comfort. Spending time in God's Word builds my trust in God's love, which will be the sustaining comfort in the storms ahead. My many heart wounds, trials, and offenses to forgive have required me to become a valedictorian of God's Word; otherwise, believe me, I would be one of the biggest cynics around.

God's Word allows us to live internally within a circle of quiet amid a clamoring evil world. "How blessed the man you train, GOD, the woman you instruct in your Word, providing a circle of quiet within the clamor of evil" (Ps. 94:12–13 THE MESSAGE).

Have you already developed the discipline of spending daily time in God's Word? By developing this holy habit, your heart simultaneously develops a capacity to begin rewriting its auto-biography in a context of hope. The psalmist wrote, "If your law [Word] had not been my delight, I would have perished in my affliction" (Ps. 119:92).

Even in the furnace of Job's suffering, he remarked that God's Word was enormously precious to his soul. Through the many years before I learned how to forgive and become a freed hostage, I, like Job, was sustained and kept from breaking through a holy habit of time in God's Word.

> He knows the way that I take;
>   when he has tested me,
> I will come forth as gold.
> ... I have not departed from the
>   commands of his lips;
> I have treasured the words of his mouth
>   more than my daily bread. (Job 23:10, 12)

I am convinced that Job came forth as gold in his horrific trial because the words of God's mouth were the life-giving poetry of his soul. Job could use the mighty tool of praying blessings on his offensive friends because his deep faith gave him the strength to pick up this forgiveness tool. We need to spend time thinking about God's Word rather than pondering the offenses and injustices committed against us.

Out of Something Painful, Something Beautiful Grew

I had just returned home from a speaking engagement when my husband asked me to look at something in the newspaper, and a picture of a handsome young man caught my eye. The picture was of an eleven-year-old boy named Robert, who had just lost his battle with leukemia. I wept and prayed for his parents, who were now facing the enormous pain of losing their firstborn son. I asked the Lord how anyone could face such an unimaginable loss. Immediately the thought came: *By grace—for grace is the unimaginable capacity to face the unimaginable!*

As I spent the next day praying and pondering the great loss of Robert, the Lord led me to a passage about Joseph and his sons. We've seen that Joseph named his firstborn Manasseh because "God has made me forget all my trouble and all my father's household" (Gen. 41:51). *Manasseh* reflected the idea of forgetting. Joseph named his secondborn Ephraim because "God has made me fruitful in the land of my suffering" (Gen. 41:52).

In Genesis 48, Joseph brought his two sons to his father, Jacob, to bless before dying. Because Joseph's father was ill and not able to see clearly, Joseph carefully positioned Manasseh on Jacob's right, since he was the firstborn, and Ephraim on Jacob's left. A surprising thing happened:

> Israel reached out his right hand and put it on Ephraim's head, though he was the younger, and crossing his arms, he put his left hand on Manasseh's head, even though Manasseh was the firstborn....When Joseph saw his father placing his right hand on Ephraim's head he was displeased. (Gen. 48:14, 17)

Why would Jacob cross his hands and bless Ephraim above Manasseh? Why would he honor the son who made his father fruitful despite his suffering over the son who made him forget his painful past? As I pondered these questions, this answer came to my heart: while forgetting a terrible past is a great thing, producing fruit despite a painful past is a *miraculous event*. Maybe being a survivor, being a Manasseh, brings glory to the survivor, whereas being fruitful in suffering, being an Ephraim, brings glory to God, who alone can give the grace-filled capacity to face the unimaginable and be fruitful in the unimaginable. Of course, God gave Joseph the strength to "Manasseh" (forget the trouble), but a greater glory is to let suffering become a platform for the display of God's glory. Suffering gives us the cross, and the cross gives us God.

"The world tells us to run from suffering, to avoid it at all costs, to cry out to heaven to take it away. Few of us would choose to suffer. Yet when we know that God has allowed suffering into our lives for a purpose, we can embrace it instead of running from it, and we can seek God in the midst of suffering."[5] So said a woman named Nancy Guthrie, who buried two infants in three years. She has faced the unimaginable, and through God's grace has been able to live the unimaginable blessing of Ephraim.

Hanging on to yesterday will produce barrenness in my life today. When I let God "Manasseh" and "Ephraim" my yesterday, I become a well-watered garden. Everyone suffers, but not everyone forgives; therefore, not everyone is fruitful in suffering. Some of the greatest fruit to come from suffering is forgiving the unforgivable.

Ernest Hemingway wrote, "The world breaks everyone; some become strong in the broken places." Forgiveness, as we've seen, rises from strength.

Knowing How to Trust and Forgive Permits One to Face the Unimaginable

Prior to speaking at a large mother-daughter conference, I was told several of the young girls who would be attending had been molested by a staff member. The staff member would be going to trial in the next two weeks, so the past wounds were being freshly confronted.

Just prior to speaking, I came across the story of Jairus's daughter, whom Jesus called back to life after she died: *"Talitha koum!"* (Mark 5:41). Immediately the Lord spoke to my heart and said, *"Today, Jackie, you are going to call some young girls back from the dead."* At the conference, as each mother brought her daughter up to me, I prayed over each of them that Jesus would heal her heart wound—that He would call each child back from the emotionally deadening experience of abuse. Jairus's daughter was twelve years old when she was raised from the dead, and most of the little girls I prayed with were seventh graders—twelve and thirteen years old.

In the first Scripture Jesus ever read publicly, He said He came to "heal the brokenhearted" (Luke 4:18 NKJV). Isaiah also referred to Jesus as "familiar with suffering" (Isa. 53:3). Jesus' familiarity with suffering allows Him to heal the brokenhearted, and my familiarity with suffering allows me to be a wounded healer—and a healed forgiver—in His name.

Then the Lord reminded me of a term that I found while researching the name *Yeshua*—friend of the brokenhearted (see Ps. 34:18). The term is *Kardiognostes*, meaning "the heart-knower."[6] The minute I remembered this term, I saw my hand over my heart in a pledge, which would be a daily whispered prayer: "*Kardiognostes*, heal my heart wounds." I told each of the girls to place her hand over her heart and continually whisper this prayer to Jesus: "Heal my heart wound, Lord." The healing of such a wound takes time . . . I know this all too well.

At the end of the conference, as I was sitting alone at the airport, I placed my hand over my heart and pledged a new allegiance to the One who is the ultimate healer of heart wounds. While my hand was over my heart, I thanked God for the abuse that I had lived through as a child, because the suffering I had experienced became the very platform of hope that Jesus can use to call a person back from the dead—"the soul-deadening experience of sexual abuse." Before you go to sleep tonight, place your hand over your heart and ask Jesus to heal any fresh or old heart wound. "If we are distressed, it is *for your comfort and salvation*" (2 Cor. 1:6, emphasis added).

Framing One's Life with God's Sovereignty

During the last decade, I have heard Elie Wiesel quoted so often that I finally went to the store and purchased his bestselling book *Night*. This man won the Nobel Peace Prize. He went into Hitler's heinous prison-camp system at fifteen years old and actually survived to tell the world about the atrocities he witnessed. One of the most amazing stories in the book was about the Jewish men walking to their deaths, and as they were marching toward Hitler's furnace of hell, they were all repeating this phrase: "'Yisgadal, veyiskadash, shmey raba...May His name be exalted and sanctified.'"[7]

I wept as I read this whole book, but this phrase, *"May His name be exalted and sanctified,"* reflected amazing trust in God's sovereignty, even when Hitler was scheduling terrifying deaths.

King David placed his confidence in God even when being chased in the wilderness by jealous King Saul. Saul wanted David dead, and when David had two opportunities to prevail against Saul and take his life, he refused to kill him. David's response emanated from such deep trust in God's sovereignty that he spoke to Saul from a mountain ridge in front of all the soldiers, a speech demonstrating consummate trust in God's control: "If the LORD has stirred you up against me, then let him accept my offering. But if this is simply a human scheme, then may those involved be cursed by the LORD" (1 Sam. 26:19 NLT).

Trust in God's sovereignty will eventually bring us to a place where we will actually learn to be grateful for our scars as well as our blessings. Through living the principle that gratitude transforms suffering into a gift, I have learned to choose by faith to give thanks in everything. "The pain I have endured has made me the woman I am. And the more gratitude I find in my heart for the pain I have suffered, even unjustly, the more my life seems to matter."[8]

For several years I attended a Bible study on Tuesdays. For more than a year, a particular woman would always have a cynical response to any comment on God's promises or goodness or love. I considered not going to the Bible study because her cynical remarks seemed too toxic for my recovering soul. Every time I told my mentor that I would not be returning because of this woman's hopeless remarks, she would always pep-talk me into attending one more week.

One unforgettable Tuesday this woman arrived with such joy on her face, I honestly thought she had been to a plastic surgeon. We all noticed her joy, and I will never forget her reply when I asked her what had happened. She read this passage:

> This is what the LORD of Heaven's Armies, the God of Israel, says to all the captives he has exiled to Babylon from Jerusalem: Build homes, and plan to stay. Plant gardens, and eat the food you produce. Marry and have children. Then find spouses for them so that you may have many grandchildren. Multiply! *Do not dwindle away!* (Jer. 29:4–6 NLT, emphasis added)

She then proceeded to share how God showed her that she had been clinging to unforgiveness. This revelation delivered her from bitter captivity. God showed her that no matter what her circumstances in life, she did not have to let her life dwindle away. She could even plant a garden in captivity. We all began to cheer at this revelation given to her through God's Word.

Sometimes you may feel that you are still a hostage to yesterday when facing so many buried offenses. Consider this: when you dig up what you have buried (an inevitable process when forgiving)—clear the soil! Then you can plant a garden where your pain used to be. That will be your Ephraim story.

Optimism/Hope Flows from Confidence in God's Sovereignty

A radio host once said to me: "Jackie, I know that you and I are kindred spirits theologically. We believe in the sovereignty of God and the providence of God. How do you balance the two, the providence of God, God's sovereignty, and what happened to you? Isn't that a difficult thing to juggle?"

I told her that once you get your faith bigger than your need to know why, the bitterness and anger can start subsiding. When your trust becomes stronger, you actually get to a place where you don't ask why anymore; instead, you say, "Okay, Lord, what do You want me to learn from this? Whom can I be a blessing to? How can I live the blessing? You instruct me."

Even though my beloved counselor M. E. Cravens didn't have extensive training in sexual abuse recovery, she was an expert in developing trust. As I learned more to trust God, then I became able to take the big step of trusting Him with the outcome of this horrible thing that He had permitted. That little word *trust* has kept me going for forty years. Why doesn't matter anymore. Now I just say, "Whatever, Father! You write the script. I know You're going to bring good. I've lived long enough to know that You bring good out of horrible things."

Consider what Solomon wrote: "Crying is better than laughing. It blotches the face but it scours the heart. Sages invest themselves in hurt and grieving. Fools waste their lives in fun and games" (Eccl. 7:3–4 THE MESSAGE).

Addiction to Hope Begins

In order to walk in the principles that you have just read about in the previous chapters, you need not only the development of faith and trust but also the support staff of perseverance. Perseverance is actually produced through suffering; and when a person perseveres in suffering, character is enhanced and hope is fortified. In fact, persevering in suffering produces an addiction to hope. I am a "hope junkie"! This is a biblical reality, not just an experiential conclusion:

> We rejoice in the hope of the glory of God. Not only so, but we also rejoice in our sufferings, because we know that suffering produces perseverance; perseverance, character; and character, hope. And *hope does not disappoint us*, because God has poured out his love into our hearts by the Holy Spirit, whom he has given us. (Rom. 5:2–5, emphasis added)

When difficult times come, do not fear suffering! These tough times just qualify you as a candidate for persevering hope. You are ready to become a hope junkie. Furthermore, an additional bonus of perseverance is that perseverance produces character—that means revealing your authentic Christianity. Too many people spend tremendous amounts of energy trying to *escape* a trial rather than using that energy to *persevere* in the trial.

People who are addicted to hope have a reality-based attitude about each day. It's like the quote a friend sent me: "Patience is accepting a difficult situation without giving God a deadline to remove it." Hope addicts have grasped the warning Jesus gave

His disciples in John 16: "I have told you this, so that when the time comes you will remember that I warned you. I did not tell you this at first because I was with you" (16:4). Jesus warned His beloved disciples that suffering was coming. What does forewarning have to do with addiction to hope? Surprise suffering can seduce us away from our hope in Jesus. Surprise suffering can temporarily impair our spiritual focus when we are not fortified with hope. Forewarning sets up safe boundaries around our suffering so that we are not craftily seduced through the surprise of the painful event. Just the other day I was mumbling to myself—"Yep, another chance to forgive him (my husband)." My husband asked me, "What did you just say?" I told him, "Another chance to practice what I teach and write—forgive again." And he laughed and said, "I have given you plenty of practice."

Hope allowed Sophia to forgive the unforgivable. Here is her story:

> *On September 25, 2002, my mother was murdered. The killer was a homeless family friend we allowed to live at our house until he got back on his feet. My parents helped out many people, especially Vietnamese refugees, by giving them a place to stay, teaching them how to drive, and helping them find a job. The day my mother died, I had three exams, and normally I went home right away after school to sleep. For some reason, I decided to go to work. After I'd worked for about an hour, my mother called and said she was leaving and she was going to pick up [Sophia's sister] Tina [who was at home sleeping]. A few hours later, I received a phone call from my mother's best friend, who frantically told me my mom had been shot and she heard my mom scream. I jumped in the car. As I was driving, I*

thought about Tina and tried to call her. Finally, when I was five minutes away from home, Tina picked up. I asked if she was okay and she said she just wakened from a nap. I asked her to go check on Mom.

She found my mom on her bed, lifeless. She'd been shot twice. When I got home, I ran to my mom's room and hugged my mother, though I knew she was gone. Then the police and ambulance came. During that time, I prayed and surrendered to God completely, knowing that life would be completely different from then on.

Prior to this loss, Sophia had learned the principles in this book. When her mother was killed, she courageously began the journey of not only forgiving her mother's killer, but forgiving also a relative who sexually abused her. She said,

God taught me to forgive even when there's no apology. My spiritual mother taught me to choose in my mind to forgive and the heart would follow. That was the first time I was released from this nightmare, because for years, I held on to offenses and refused to forgive unless the person expressed remorse. Many people ask how I went about forgiving my mother's murderer. When I think back on how God has taken me step-by-step [through the process of forgiveness], I realize that this new trial was difficult, but not impossible.

Sophia is a heroic forgiver, and a woman who is free to love!

An addiction to hope is developed. You may begin as a cynic but then move to become a hope-filled follower of Jesus. Erwin McManus spoke at a conference in Arizona, where I heard him define himself as "a cynic who believes." Everyone laughed, but

I heard his vulnerable candor and knew he had traveled many miles on this journey of addiction to hope. But we can still believe there is hope in Jesus. Of course this is possible only if we build our faith in God.

God's sovereignty is not some dusty old doctrine for theologians. It is for everyday people. The belief that God is in control and attentive to our lives 24/7 is a must for anyone who wants to forgive and love. The only way I won't become stuck in the *Diary of Why* is if I allow the portrait of my life to be placed in the frame of God's sovereignty. The hook that fastens my portrait to the frame of sovereignty is trust—which ultimately produces hope. I once read a book jacket that said, "The ability to find meaning and hope in suffering offers a powerful secret to mental health and survival."[9]

Did you notice the phrase "powerful secret to mental health"? The health of our souls and minds is inextricably linked to finding meaning and hope in suffering. Because of Jesus and the capacity to forgive—we *can* find hope and meaning even in a multitude of offenses.

Hope Continues to Thrive—
Forgiveness Continues to Flow

On the day of an incredible teaching opportunity, I was struggling more than I had anticipated. I decided to spend some more time in the Word, hoping to calm my restless heart. I came upon this familiar verse: "Simon, Simon, Satan has asked to sift you as wheat. But I have prayed for you, Simon, that your faith may not fail. And when you have turned back, strengthen your brothers" (Luke 22:31–32).

The phrase "Satan has asked" jumped out at me, and I

looked up the word *asked*. In the Greek it means "insistent request, craving demand."[10] When I thought about the struggle my soul was facing, I thought about Satan insistently demanding the opportunity to sift me like wheat. I could see him pounding a desk, demanding a chance to shake my world. As that thought passed through my heart, a cold chill moved over my body.

Then I read the part of the verse where Jesus said, "But I have prayed for you, Simon." I teared up and said, "Jesus, what have You prayed for me today?" Hebrews states that Jesus is our High Priest who lives to make intercession for us (see 7:25), but my heart wanted more. I wanted to hear Jesus say, "But I have prayed for *you*, Jackie. I know you are struggling today. I know that Satan is trying to stir up a storm in your soul. But I have prayed for you." As I spoke my heart's desire out loud to God, the Lord brought to my mind John 17: "They are still in the world, and I am coming to you. Holy Father, protect them by the power of your name, the name you gave me.... While I was with them, I protected them and kept them safe by that name you gave me" (vv. 11–12).

As I was dissecting the words in this verse, I couldn't wait to look up the word *protect* in Greek. I found it means "to watch, guard, keep an eye on."[11] When I read "keep an eye on," the One who prayed this verse said, *"Two thousand years ago I asked the Father to keep an eye on you!"*

I literally came out of the chair I was sitting in with a shout of joy. Two thousand years ago, Jesus prayed for me in the garden. Two thousand years ago, He asked the Father to keep an eye on me. The Father is the Guardian, the Keeper of my soul. Satan may regularly demand a shot at stirring things up in my life, but I know that I have been prayed for, and, consequently, my faith will not fail.

May the phrase "I've asked the Father to keep an eye on you" be a comfort and a strength whenever you hear the enemy pounding his fist and causing a disturbance in your life through a fresh offense that will need forgiveness. Don't let the enemy outwit you and intimidate your desire to have the identity of one who forgives freely, because of Jesus.

Separation Anxiety

As I close this last chapter, I am actually experiencing "reader/ author separation anxiety." If I could meet you for coffee, I would want to encourage you one more time — "Don't let the enemy keep you bound and gagged via unforgiveness! Let your faith grow. Use the tools I offer you." I would want to ask, "Does forgiving and forgiving again still seem like a ludicrous request?" My heart's prayer is that you consider the reality that Satan has desired to outwit you through unforgiveness, but Jesus has prayed for you and He has been keeping an eye on you. May that thought help you by faith to pull the gag out of your mouth and declare that you want to be a person identified as *one who forgives*. Having been forgiven by faith, you have the capacity to be a champion forgiver by faith. Those who choose daily to be good forgivers "bring honor to Christ" (2 Cor. 8:23 NLT).

Remember: the core of emotional health is inextricably linked to the ability to forgive. Take these principles and begin a freedom march away from yesterday's captivity and into God's glorious plan for your future — it is within your reach!

This freedom march of forgiveness will allow you to finally love freely, even those who have previously seemed unlovable. As Mother Teresa once said,

People ask me what advice I have for a married couple struggling in their relationship. I always answer: pray and forgive. And to young people from violent homes, I say pray and forgive. And even to the single mother with no family support: pray and forgive.[12]

I have a dream…that hundreds of thousands of my spiritual siblings will join this freedom march of forgiveness. On the cross more than two thousand years ago, Jesus Christ cried, "It is finished" (John 19:30), and then He died for all mankind. When He rose from the dead, He became the leader of this freedom march of forgiveness.

MAKE IT PERSONAL

1. What past heart wounds need the hope and healing of God's Word?
2. Do you think that spending more time learning God's Word will help with hope deprivation?
3. Are you still stuck in relation to forgiving a particular person and a specific offense? Revisit Jeremiah 29:4–5 and ponder the possibility of letting life dwindle away in your "stuck" condition.
4. Do you have a daily Bible-reading habit established in your life? If not, what has prevented its development? (See Job 23:10, 12.)
5. Is it still a stretch for you to accept the Ephraim message: out of something painful, something beautiful grew? (See Gen. 41:51, 52; 48:14–17.)

6. How can these verses help you reframe past hurt in the sovereignty of God? Think of an example for each.

- God stoops down to give me strength (see Neh. 8:10).
- God stoops down to make the way clear for me (see Ps. 18:32).
- God stoops down to train me for life's battles (see Ps. 144:1).
- God stoops down to give me light so I can walk through the darkest night (see Job 29:3).
- God stoops down to give me the capacity to scale the walls people build (see Ps. 18:29).
- God stoops down in delight to rescue me (see Ps. 18:19).
- God stoops down to confide in me (see Ps. 25:14).
- God stoops down to bless me in the sight of men (see Ps. 31:19).
- God stoops down to place a song in the heart of a former "slime pit dweller" (see Ps. 40:2).
- God stoops down to quiet my anxious heart with His love (see Zeph. 3:17).
- God stoops down to keep me from hurting myself (see Ps. 18:36).
- God stoops down to sustain me (see Ps. 119:116).

Appendix

Recommended Reading for the Soon-to-Be-Released Hostage!

(This is in addition to your daily reading of God's Word.)

Red Circle Project: Take a red pencil and read through the Psalms, circling the word *trust* wherever you see it.

Building Trust

Bridges, Jerry. *Trusting God: Even When Life Hurts*. Colorado Springs, CO: NavPress, 1988.

Crabb, Larry. *Shattered Dreams: God's Unexpected Pathway to Joy*. Colorado Springs, CO: Waterbrook, 2001.

Lucado, Max. *In the Eye of the Storm: A Day in the Life of Jesus*. Dallas, TX: Word, 1991.

Yancy, Philip. *Disappointment with God: Three Questions No One Asks Aloud*. New York: Walker, 2000.

Devotion to God

Chambers, Oswald. *My Utmost for His Highest*. Grand Rapids, MI: Discovery House, 1989.

Edwards, Gene. *Exquisite Agony: Experiencing the Cross as Seen from the Father.* Jacksonville, FL: Seed Sowers, 1994.

Elliot, Elisabeth. *Passion and Purity: Learning to Bring Your Love Life Under Christ's Control.* Old Tappan, NJ: Revell, 2002.

Foster, Robert. *Celebration of Discipline: The Path to Spiritual Growth.* San Francisco, CA: Harper San Francisco, 1998.

Lord, Peter. *Soul Care.* Grand Rapids, MI: Baker Books, 1990.

Manning, Brennan. *Abba's Child: The Cry of the Heart for Intimate Belonging.* Colorado Springs, CO: NavPress, 2002.

Myers, Ruth. *31 Days of Praise: Enjoying God Anew.* Sisters, OR: Multnomah, 2005.

Tozer, A. W. *Pursuit of God: The Human Thirst for the Divine.* Harrisburg, PA: Christian Publications, 1982.

Building a Healthy Self-Image

Cloud, Dr. Henry and John Townsend. *Boundaries: When to Say Yes, When to Say No to Take Control of Your Life.* Grand Rapids, MI: Zondervan, 2002.

McGee, Robert. *The Search for Significance: Seeing Your True Worth Through God's Eyes.* Nashville, TN: Thomas Nelson, 2003.

Seamands, David. *Healing Grace: Finding Freedom from the Performance Trap.* Colorado Springs, CO: Cook Communications, 1991.

Smedes, Lewis. *Shame and Grace: Healing the Shame We Don't Deserve.* New York: Harper One, 1994.

Wilson, Sandra. *The World According to Me: Recognizing and Releasing our Illusions of Control.* Colorado Springs, CO: Cook Communications, 1995.

Grace

Fischer, John. *12 Steps for the Recovering Pharisee (Like Me): Finding Grace to Live Unmasked.* Grand Rapids, MI: Bethany House, 2000.

Yancey, Dr. Philip. *What's So Amazing About Grace?* Grand Rapids, MI: Zondervan, 2002.

Parenting

Cline, Foster and Jim Faye. *Parenting with Love and Logic: Teaching Children Responsibility.* Colorado Springs, CO: Piñon Press, 2006.

Smalley, Gary. *Key to Your Child's Heart: Raise Motivated, Obedient, and Loving Children.* Nashville, TN: Thomas Nelson, 2003.

Van Vonderen, Jeff. *Families Where Grace Is in Place: Getting Free from the Burden of Pressuring, Controlling, and Manipulating Your Spouse and Children.* Grand Rapids, MI: Bethany House, 1992. [out of print]

Sexual Abuse Recovery

Allender, Dan. *Wounded Heart: Hope for Adult Victims of Childhood Sexual Abuse.* Colorado Springs, CO: NavPress, 1995.

Gil, Dr. Eliana. *Outgrowing the Pain: A Book for and About Adults Abused as Children.* New York: Dell, 1988.

Van Stone, Doris and Erwin W. Lutzer. *No Place to Cry: The Hurt and Healing.* Chicago, IL: Moody, 1992.

Notes

Introduction

1. Brennan Manning, *The Importance of Being Foolish* (San Francisco: HarperSanFrancisco, 2005), 25.

1. Counterfeit Forgiveness

1. Gwin Turner, *The Heritage Bible*, http://www.cathedraluniversity.com/heritagebible/index.asp, 1801.

2. *Strong's Exhaustive Concordance* (McLean, VA: MacDonald Publishing Company, 1972), #3540 and #3559.

3. *The American Heritage Dictionary*, s.v. "offense."

4. Miroslav Volf, *Exclusion and Embrace* (Nashville, TN: Abingdon Press, 1996), 235, emphasis added.

5. Jill Smolowe and Gail Westcott, "She Shared a Dream," *People*, February 13, 2006, 94.

6. Paul Tournier, *The Gift of Feeling* (Atlanta: John Knox Press 1979), 107.

7. JoAnne Kaufman, "Forgive Me," *Good Housekeeping*, November 2004, 174.

8. *Strong's*, #3513.

9. Ibid., #863.

10. N. Bustani, "Resolving Conflict the Healthy Way" (1999 Seminar notes, not published).

2. Held Hostage by Shame

1. Poem by Leslie Davies (not published); used by permission.

2. *Strong's*, #4834.

3. Lewis B. Smedes, *Shame and Grace* (New York: HarperCollins Publishers, 1993).

4. A. W. Tozer quoted in John Eldredge, *Waking the Dead* (Nashville, TN: Thomas Nelson Publishers, 2003), 154.

5. Peter Lord, *Soul Care* (Grand Rapids: Baker Book House, 1990), 21.

6. Henri Nouwen, *Discipleship* magazine, issue 100, 1997, 75.

3. Authentic Forgiveness

1. *The Oxford American College Dictionary*, s.v. "for" and "give."

2. Richard Foster and James Smith, *Devotional Classics* (San Francisco: HarperSanFrancisco, 1991), 69.

3. Volf, *Exclusion and Embrace*, 126–28.

4. *Strong's*, #4348.

5. *Hebrew-Greek Key Word Study Bible* (Chattanooga, TN: AMG Publishers, 1996), #5953.

4. Held Hostage by the Size of the Offense

1. Tony Carnes, "Jesus in Istanbul" and Denise McGill, "A Victorious Family," *Christianity Today*, January 2008, 25, 28, 29.

2. *Strong's*, #630.

3. Ibid., #863.

4. *Hebrew-Greek Key Word Study Bible*, #6143.

5. Held Hostage by Assaulting Memories

1. *Archaeological Study Bible* (Grand Rapids: Zondervan, 2005), 1593.

2. Jesse Sandberg, *Letting People Off the Hook* (Wheaton, IL: Victor Books, 1995), 116.

3. David Seamands, *Putting Away Childish Things* (Wheaton, IL: Victor Books, 1982), 19.

4. Immaculée Ilibagiza with Steve Erwin, *Left to Tell* (Carlsbad, CA: Hay House Inc., 2006), 232.

6. Held Hostage by Repeated Offense

1. *Hebrew-Greek Key Word Study Bible*, #3357.

2. *Strong's*, #5201.

3. Ruth Olsen, e-mail message to author.

4. *Strong's*, #2254.

5. Lynda Thomas, e-mail message to author, 2007.

6. Jan Silvious, *Look At It This Way* (Colorado Springs: Waterbrook-Press, 2003), 10, 12, emphasis added.

7. John Piper, *Dangerous Duty of Delight* (Sisters, OR: Multnomah Publishers, 2001).

8. Quoted in Donald Miller and John MacMurray, *To Own A Dragon* (Colorado Springs: NavPress, 2006), 191–92.

9. Oswald Chambers, *My Utmost for His Highest* (Grand Rapids: Discovery House, 1989), May 16.

10. Brennan Manning, *Ruthless Trust* (New York: HarperCollins, 2000).

11. Sermon: "The Suffering of Christ and the Sovereignty of God," www.DesiringGod.com/sermon 228, 3.

7. Held Hostage by Revenge Fantasies

1. Mary Lou White, correspondence with author, 2006.

2. *Hebrew-Greek Key Word Study Bible*, Lexical Aids, #2895, p. 1638.

3. *Strong's*, #2095 and #3056.

4. *Hebrew-Greek Key Word Study Bible*, Lexical Aids, #5746.

5. Francis Frangipane, "Unoffendable, Part I," June 14, 2007, http://frangipane.org.

6. Peter Ames Carlin, "Anniversary Article" on Hemingway's death, *People*, July 12, 1999, 146–48.

7. Bob Meadow, Paysha Rhone, and Tom Duffy, "I Forgive You," *People*, May 8, 2006, 199.

8. Volf, *Exclusion and Embrace*, 124.

9. *Strong's*, #7503.

10. *The Heritage Bible*, http://www.cathedraluniversity.com/heritagebible/index.asp.

11. Charles Colson, *Loving God* (New York: Harper Paperbacks, 1983).

8. Held Hostage by the Incubation of Anger

1. Frederick Buechner, *Wishful Thinking: A Seeker's ABC* (New York: HarperCollins, 2001).

2. *Strong's*, #5117.

3. "Problem Anger and What We Can Do About It," *The Boiling Point*, http://www.mentalhealth.org.uk/campaigns/anger-and-mental-health/boiling-point-report/.

4. *Strong's*, #4834.

5. Wynn Free with Fred Luskin, "Forgiveness: It's Good for Your Health," *The Spirit of Mast* magazine, November 2002.

6. *Strong's*, #7356, #2963, #8104.

9. Forgiveness Tool of Praying Blessings
on the Offender

1. Gordon MacDonald, *The Resilient Life* (Nashville, TN: Thomas Nelson, 2004), 129.

2. *The Heritage Bible*, http://www.cathedraluniversity.com/heritagebible/index.asp.

3. "Social Intelligence," *Reader's Digest*, February 2007, 129, emphasis added; this is excerpted from Daniel Goleman, *Social Intelligence* (UK: Random House, 2006).

4. Karin Evans, "Forgive and Forget," advertising supplement, reprinted for *Health* magazine, 2001.

5. Kristin Armstrong, *Happily Ever After* (Nashville, TN: FaithWords, 2007), 38.

6. Helen Kooiman Hoiser, *100 Christian Women Who Changed the 20th Century* (Grand Rapids: Fleming H. Revell, 2000).

7. *The Heritage Bible*, http://www.cathedraluniversity.com/heritagebible/index.asp, 1892.

10. Forgiveness Tool of Exposing
Unrealistic Expectations

1. Anne Lamott, *Blue Shoes*, book on tape (Riverhead Books/Penguin USA, 2002).

2. *Strong's*, #4085.

3. Ibid., #3709.

4. Ibid., # 4478 and #4100.

5. Francis Frangipane, "Unoffendable, Part II," June 22, 2007, http://frangipane.org.

6. Chambers, *My Utmost for His Highest*, May 16; Aug. 10.

7. *Strong's*, #3925.

8. John Garrity, "Tiger," *Sports Illustrated*, April 2, 2007, 70.

11. Forgiveness Tool of Growing Faith

1. *Strong's*, #5341.

2. Ibid., #7931.

3. Barri Cae Mallin and Shmuel Wolkenfeld, *Intimate Moments with the Hebrew Names of God* (Gainesville, FL: Bridge-Logos Publishers, 2001), 136.

4. Jerry Bridges, *Trusting God* (Colorado Springs: NavPress, 1988).

5. Nancy Guthrie, *Holding on to Hope* (Wheaton, IL: Tyndale House, 2004).

6. *Strong's*, #2840 and #1108.

7. Elie Wiesel, *Night* (New York: Hill and Wang, 1958), 33.

8. Leslie Parrott, *You Matter More Than You Think* (Grand Rapids: Zondervan, 2006), 46.

9. Viktor E. Frankl, *Man's Search for Meaning* (New York: Simon & Schuster, 1959), 17.

10. *Strong's*, #1809.

11. Ibid., #5083.

12. See www.writespirit.net/inspirational_quotes.

About the Author

Jackie Kendall has been a sought-after conference speaker for twenty-five years. As president of Power to Grow Ministries, Jackie speaks to people of all ages and stages of life (including, since 1992, professional baseball and football players). Jackie is the author of several books, and the coauthor of the bestselling *Lady in Waiting*.

For speaking engagements or to get more information, contact Jackie at:

Power to Grow Ministries
www.jackiekendall.com